Pearson Revise

Pearson Edexcel GCSE (9–1)
History
The USA, 1954–75: conflict at home and abroad
Revision Guide and Workbook

Series Consultant: Harry Smith

Author: Victoria Payne

A note from the publisher

In order to ensure that this resource offers high-quality support for the associated Pearson qualification, it has been through a review process by the awarding body. This process confirms that this resource fully covers the teaching and learning content of the specification or part of a specification at which it is aimed. It also confirms that it demonstrates an appropriate balance between the development of subject skills, knowledge and understanding, in addition to preparation for assessment.

Endorsement does not cover any guidance on assessment activities or processes (e.g. practise questions or advice on how to answer assessment questions), included in the resource nor does it prescribe any particular approach to the teaching or delivery of a related course.

While the publishers have made every attempt to ensure that advice on the qualification and its assessment is accurate, the official specification and associated assessment guidance materials are the only authoritative source of information and should always be referred to for definitive guidance.

Pearson examiners have not contributed to any sections in this resource relevant to examination papers for which they have responsibility.

Examiners will not use endorsed resources as a source of material for any assessment set by Pearson.

Endorsement of a resource does not mean that the resource is required to achieve this Pearson qualification, nor does it mean that it is the only suitable material available to support the qualification, and any resource lists produced by the awarding body shall include this and other appropriate resources.

For the full range of Pearson revision titles across KS2, 11+, KS3, GCSE, Functional Skills, AS/A Level and BTEC visit:

www.pearsonschools.co.uk/revise

Contents

. . . .

A small bit of small print

Edexcel publishes Sample Assessment Material and the Specification on its website. This is the official content and this book should be used in conjunction with it. The questions in *Now try this* have been written to help you practise every topic in the book. Remember: the real exam questions may not look like this.

The early 1950s

Across the USA in the 1950s, black Americans were treated as second-class citizens. In the South they faced **segregation, discrimination** and attempts to prevent them from voting. Organisations such as the NAACP and CORE campaigned to improve black civil rights.

Segregation and discrimination in the Southern states

Racial segregation in the South in the early 1950s aimed to prevent black and white Americans mixing on public transport and in schools, restaurants and other public places.

Racist 'Jim Crow' laws were used to segregate black and white Americans.

The law stated that it was legal to segregate as long as services were 'separate but equal'.

Segregated public facilities and services included cinemas, toilets, schools and transport.

In reality, services for black Americans were often inferior to those for white people.

Turn to page 2 to find out more about the principle of 'separate but equal'.

Students protest to keep schools segregated in Baltimore, Maryland, in 1955.

Discrimination and violence in the Southern states

- The majority of white people viewed black Americans as racially inferior.
- Racist white officials, including police and judges, were often members of the Ku Klux Klan.
- The frequent assaults and murders of black people were not properly investigated or prosecuted.
- Black people were not allowed to sit on juries in a court of law.

Go to page 6 to find out more about the Ku Klux Klan.

CORE and the NAACP made more progress in the Northern states, where they had more white support. Both organisations were racially integrated.

Voting rights

- White gangs physically stopped black Americans from voting, and sometimes attacked them for trying to register to vote.
- Some Southern states, such as Georgia and Virginia, passed laws making it harder for black people to vote. For example, they used unfair literacy tests to make it harder for black Americans to qualify for the vote.
- Some Southern states introduced the 'grandfather clause' whereby voters had to prove their forefathers had voted. For descendants of slaves this was impossible as they had been barred from voting.
- Sometimes white employers sacked black workers if they registered to vote or voted.

Civil rights organisations

NAACP (National Association for the Advancement of Colored People)	CORE (Congress of Racial Equality)
• It was set up in 1909. • They fought for civil rights using the legal system and the courts. • They defended black people who had been unfairly convicted of crimes. • It focused on overturning 'separate but equal' ruling.	• It was set up in 1942. • They had a smaller membership than NAACP. • Members used **non-violent direct action**; they trained local activists in these techniques. • They operated mostly in Northern states. • In early years of the organisation, most members were white and middle class.

Now try this

Complete a table with 'Bad treatment of black Americans in the early 1950s' in the left column and 'Organised resistance to bad treatment' in the right column. Add at least **three** points to each column.

Brown v. Topeka, 1954

In 1952, the NAACP put five desegregation cases together and took them to the Supreme Court as Brown versus the Board of Education, Topeka, Kansas – otherwise known as *Brown v. Topeka*.

Key features of *Brown v. Topeka*

My name is Linda Brown. I am a black American student who became famous after my experiences of segregated school education were used in a legal case brought to the Supreme Court by the NAACP in 1954. The legal case was made against the Topeka Board of Education. It argued that the principle of **'separate but equal'** in schools was **unconstitutional**, as it damaged black children. In the case, a key point was that I had to walk past my local white school to reach the nearest black school. Segregated schools made me feel separate and not equal to white kids.

In 1896, the Supreme Court ruled that racial segregation was constitutional as long as facilities were 'separate but equal'. However, conditions for black Americans were often separate and unequal. For example, black schools were often underfunded compared to white schools and had poor facilities.

For more information on the situation of black Americans in the Southern states in the early 1950s, turn to page 1.

Linda Brown, photographed outside the school in Topeka, 10 years after the legal case was first made.

Timeline

Brown v. Topeka, 1954

Dec 1952 The judges in the case asked to hear more legal advice. Earl Warren became new Chief Justice.

May 1954 The Supreme Court ruled that segregated education was unconstitutional. However, the Court set no time limit for the desegregation of schools.

May 1955 A second court ruling said that **desegregation** in schools should happen 'with all deliberate speed'.

1952 NAACP took school segregation cases to the Supreme Court, claiming segregated schools broke the **14th Amendment** (which includes clauses on citizenship and equal protection) as they made black children feel inferior.

July 1954 In the 'Deep South' (including Alabama, Georgia, Louisiana, Mississippi and South Carolina), White Citizens' Councils were set up to stop desegregation. They were prepared to use extreme violence.

1957 723 school districts had desegregated education.

Short-term significance

- *Brown* rulings overturned the 1896 *Plessy v. Ferguson* decision, which allowed public facilities, including schools, to be segregated.
- There was a white backlash and membership of the Ku Klux Klan increased.
- Black students and teachers, and their families, faced threats and hostility in desegregated schools.
- Some good schools for black Americans were shut down.
- Many Southern states found ways to avoid complying with the court rulings.

Long-term significance

- Awareness of civil rights issues in the Southern states increased.
- Rulings were an inspiration for other desegregation campaigns.
- White Americans moved out of areas where black Americans lived, to avoid forced desegregation.

Desegregation: process of replacing racial segregation with racial integration.

Now try this

Write **one** short paragraph to explain the long-term significance of the *Brown* case.

Little Rock High School, 1957

In 1957, at Little Rock High School in Little Rock, Arkansas, nine black students – known as the 'Little Rock Nine' – attended the newly desegregated high school. They were treated very badly by white Americans who wanted the segregation of schools to continue in the South.

The 'Little Rock Nine'

Following the *Brown* verdict, a decision was made for school desegregation in Little Rock.

About 75 black students applied to join Little Rock High School; the school board accepted 25. However, their families were intimidated with threats if they tried to take their places at the school. At the start of the 1957 school year, just nine students were still planning to register. These students were called the 'Little Rock Nine' by the campaigners who took up their cause.

Governor Orval Faubus

After the 1954 *Brown* verdict, Orval Faubus, state governor of Arkansas, became a fierce opponent of school integration.

In 1958, Faubus closed every school in Little Rock, in an attempt to stop racial integration taking place. This lasted for a year but pressure from parents eventually forced him to reopen schools.

Events at Little Rock, 1957

1. The *Brown* case led to the school board agreeing that Little Rock High School would be desegregated on 3 September 1957, at the start of the new school term.
2. The NAACP arranged for the new black students to arrive there together on 4 September.
3. Faubus sent 250 state troops to surround the school when the Little Rock Nine were due to start; he said this was to 'keep the peace'. This blocked the black students from gaining entrance.
4. Elizabeth Eckford did not get the notification to arrive with the rest of the group. She was targeted by the crowd and racially abused.
5. District judges and lawyers for the NAACP used the courts to challenge Faubus and force him to withdraw the state troops.
6. On 24 September, President Eisenhower sent in federal troops, to ensure black students could attend school without being attacked. The black students were finally able to enter the school successfully.

Seventeen year-old Elizabeth Eckford is followed by an aggressive crowd as she tries to enter Little Rock High School, 4 September 1957.

Presidential intervention

Worldwide media coverage of the events at Little Rock High School forced President Eisenhower to get involved, as the USA's image was being damaged abroad.

Rioting outside Little Rock High after Arkansas state troops were removed led Eisenhower to send in 1000 federal troops. Eisenhower used a presidential order, as he knew Congress would disapprove of the decision to intervene in state affairs. While he wanted to avoid using federal powers, he was concerned about white opposition to integration. Eisenhower wanted to improve black civil rights while avoiding potential violent unrest about racial integration in the Deep South, where opposition was strongest.

Significance of events at Little Rock

- Hundreds of reporters from local and international news stations reported the events. People were shocked by the coverage of how children were being racially abused.
- There was continued resistance to school integration after 1957. In the South, many schools shut down rather than desegregate.
- The first black student graduated from Little Rock High School in 1958, but fellow white students refused to sit with him at the ceremony.
- Even 10 years later, black students attending newly integrated Southern schools were subjected to violence, intimidation and exclusion by teachers and peers.

Now try this

Give **three** ways in which Little Rock was important in the campaign for desegregation.

The Montgomery Bus Boycott, 1955

On 1 December 1955, a black woman called Rosa Parks broke segregation laws in Montgomery, Alabama, by refusing to give up her seat on a bus to a white person. She was arrested and fined. Parks' decision sparked a mass boycott of the buses by those campaigning for civil rights.

Causes of the boycott

Long-term causes	Short-term causes
• The Women's Political Council in Montgomery had focused on bus discrimination since 1950. • The Montgomery bus company discriminated against black passengers by forcing them to sit at the back of buses and vacate their seats for white people. • Requests to the bus company to change their rules were not listened to.	• On 1 December 1955, Rosa Parks refused to give up her seat in the 'black' area of a bus to a white man who had no seat. • Police arrested and charged Parks under Montgomery's segregation laws.

Events of the boycott, 1955–56

For more on Martin Luther King and his role in the civil rights movement, turn to pages 5 and 6.

- **5 December 1955:** civil rights activists in Montgomery met to discuss a boycott of the city buses. They formed the Montgomery Improvement Association (MIA) and elected Martin Luther King as their chairman.
- **8 December:** the MIA met bus company officials, who refused to change the segregation on their buses. The MIA decided to continue the boycott until they won. They decided that no black Americans would use the bus service until the situation changed.
- The MIA held meetings with church groups and other organisations to plan car sharing. The first car pools began on **12 December** and grew to involve over 300 cars.
- The MIA also negotiated reduced cab fares with black drivers to enable boycotters to travel by taxi for the price of a standard bus fare.
- As the boycott continued, opposition grew. On **30 January 1956**, Martin Luther King's home was bombed. King responded by calling for peaceful protest and no retaliation.
- The violence in response to the peaceful protest increased media coverage of the boycott; media reports were largely sympathetic to the civil rights campaigners.
- Non-violent direct action was emerging as a clear and effective campaigning approach.

Significance of Rosa Parks

Rosa Parks' refusal to accept segregation on Montgomery's buses triggered a successful desegregation campaign that spurred on other civil rights activists.

Parks was a married, middle-aged woman. It was difficult to criticise her for bad behaviour or not being respectable.

She understood the principles of non-violent direct action.

She had already been involved in campaigns for black voter registration.

She was secretary of the Montgomery NAACP.

Rosa Parks making a civil rights speech a decade after the Montgomery Bus Boycott.

Now try this

1 List **three** ways that Rosa Parks was significant in the Montgomery Bus Boycott.
2 List **three** other factors that were important to the success of the boycott.

Importance of the boycott

The success of the Montgomery Bus Boycott was very important to the civil rights movement: it paved the way for further campaigns against segregation. It also brought Martin Luther King to the forefront of the civil rights movement and proved that non-violent direct action could work.

Reasons for the boycott's success

1 **Well organised.** Existing civil rights groups meant the structure was already in place to get the campaign up and running. The MIA coordinated the campaign effectively.

2 **Committed to success.** The boycott continued despite the threats the boycotters received. Some were told they would be fired from jobs and some were physically attacked; however, they were prepared to continue.

3 **Well publicised.** The campaign was publicised through church meetings and local newspapers. This helped supporters get organised and communicate with each other, to lend support.

4 **The bus company was hurt financially,** as the vast majority of its customers were black Americans, so it lost a lot of money running empty buses.

Supreme Court ruling

The NAACP brought a case to desegregate Montgomery buses. On 1 February 1956, their lawyers filed *Browder v. Gayle*, against bus segregation in Montgomery. They argued it was against the 14th Amendment because of the guarantee to equal protection.

- On 5 June, the Supreme Court ordered that segregation on buses was unconstitutional: buses should be desegregated. They gave the *Brown* decision as their reason, as it had set the precedent that segregation was unconstitutional. The bus company appealed but the appeal was rejected on 17 December.

- On 20 December, the MIA finally called off the boycott. Racially integrated bus services began on 21 December.

For details of the *Brown v. Topeka* case (1954), turn to page 2.

Significance of Martin Luther King's leadership

King was a pastor; he emphasised Christian values of love and humility.

He always advocated a non-violent approach.

King made many powerful speeches that had a huge impact on his audiences.

King tried to appeal to all Americans regardless of race – he appealed to people's shared humanity.

Martin Luther King in 1956.

He played an important part in the Montgomery Bus Boycott, helping to boost morale and raise funds for the MIA.

He was arrested in 1956 for his part in organising the boycott.

Jo Ann Gibson Robinson (civil rights activist), E.D. Nixon (civil rights campaigner and union organiser) and Ralph Abernathy (leader of the SCLC) were King's fellow campaign leaders.

The Southern Christian Leadership Conference (SCLC)

- It was set up in January 1957, to coordinate church-based protest across the South.
- It was led by Martin Luther King and Ralph Abernathy.
- Members campaigned against segregation.
- They used non-violent direct action.
- They secured black and white membership.
- The earliest major campaign was for voter registration.

The 1957 Civil Rights Act

The *Brown* case and the bus boycott led to increased public support for civil rights and a civil rights act being passed in Congress. The act aimed to increase black voter registration, make it illegal to obstruct voter registration and allow federal courts to prosecute states that did not guarantee citizen's voting rights. However, in practice, all-white juries in the South were unlikely to uphold federal prosecutions of state violations of voting rights.

Now try this

Design a concept map to show the impact of the Montgomery Bus Boycott up to 1960.

Opposition to civil rights: the KKK and violence

Black Americans in the South faced open intimidation and violence, often carried out by members of the Ku Klux Klan (KKK). Media coverage of some of these cases helped to raise awareness of the terrible injustices black Americans faced in the Southern states.

Klan members burn a cross at a rally. The KKK used this symbol to intimidate and spread fear.

Activities of the Ku Klux Klan

- Set up in 1865 after black slaves won their freedom. The KKK wanted to stop black Americans from gaining equality.
- Operated mostly in the Southern states.
- Terrorised black American families by intimidation and extreme violence, including murder, often by **lynching** (illegal execution, usually carried out by a mob).
- Only so-called WASPs (White Anglo-Saxon Protestants) could join.
- They wore hoods, as membership was secret, although in reality many Southern states' law enforcement officers were involved or sympathetic to the Klan's aims.
- Klan members also attacked Jews, Catholics and liberals, but their most extreme hatred was for black Americans.

The murder of Emmett Till, 1955

- Emmett Till, a 14-year-old black boy from Chicago, went to Mississippi in 1955 to visit family.
- Carolyn Bryant, a white woman, said that Till made sexual advances when he went to her store. Till's cousins, who were waiting outside, said he only wolf-whistled at her.
- The next night, Bryant's husband and his half-brother abducted Till and beat him severely. They shot him and threw him into the river with a weight around his neck. Till's body was found three days later.
- Till's mother had an open viewing of the body in Chicago. This led to extensive media coverage, which fuelled widespread shock and outrage, especially in the North, where many were ignorant of the treatment of black Americans in the South.
- The murder trial was reported nationwide.
- The defendants were acquitted (found not guilty). They later sold their story to a magazine, admitting to the murder.

No justice for Emmett Till

Emmett Till's family did not get justice for his murder. After the trial, black people continued to be murdered in Mississippi and the killers were rarely convicted. For example, NAACP leader George W. Lee was also murdered in 1955; his murder remains unsolved.

Media reporting of these injustices led to a public outcry and spurred on the growth of the civil rights movement.

The NAACP produced a booklet in 1955 called *M is for Mississippi and Murder*, highlighting the murders of black people in Mississippi in that year that went unpunished.

Emmett Till with his mother, Mamie Bradley, c. 1950. He was her only son.

Now try this

List **three** ways that the murder of Emmett Till was typical of the violence against black people in the 1950s.

Remember: Klan membership was secret, the KKK encouraged extreme violence against black people, and many state officials in the South were Klan members.

Political opposition to desegregation

Attempts to desegregate the South faced political opposition from national and local politicians. In addition, local people set up White Citizens' Councils to block any change.

Federal opposition to civil rights

- Attempts to introduce an effective Civil Rights Act were opposed by some Southern members of Congress.
- The 'Dixiecrats' (a splinter group from the Democratic Party made up of Southern politicians) had strong views about keeping segregation. By 1954, they had rejoined the Democrats, after previously breaking away due to disagreements about civil rights, because they believed they could have more influence from within the Democratic Party. They maintained their position on keeping segregation and protecting states' rights to retain laws that guaranteed white supremacy.
- Presidents needed the Dixiecrats' support in Congress, so had to take their views on board when creating new laws. They were fearful that the Dixiecrats would disrupt government. This hindered the cause for civil rights laws.

State opposition to civil rights

We want to keep segregation; it's our right! If federal laws force us to desegregate, we will find ways to oppose racial mixing.

The views of Southern governors and local state mayors ensured there was strong opposition to the civil rights movement and desegregation.

We only have white judges and juries in court. It's the best way to uphold justice.

Types of resistance

Some state officials resisted desegregation in the South in open ways, such as shutting down all state schools so they could not be integrated.

Other state officials used more devious ways to oppose desegregation. For example, some school admission tests were deliberately biased against black students, to prevent them from joining 'white' schools. Some states refused to end literacy tests and continued to disrupt opportunities for black voters to cast their vote at elections.

White Citizens' Councils organised protests and used threats of violence (or actual violence) against those who sought integration.

By using these underhand methods, state officials could claim to follow the letter of the law to desegregate; however, they did not stick to the spirit of desegregation laws.

White Citizens' Councils (WCC)

White Citizens' Councils were set up from 1954 onwards to stop desegregation. They had around 60000 members in the mid-1950s. They often began as organisations opposed to school desegregation in their local area after the *Brown* ruling. They opposed any desegregation, for example in libraries or swimming pools. As well as protesting and using violence, they used economic means to stop calls for desegregation: for example, in some towns WCC members sacked black employees who signed petitions or were involved in civil rights activities. Members feared that desegregation would lead to more calls for political and economic equality for black Americans.

Now try this

List **five** methods that some people used to stop desegregation in the Southern states.

Greensboro and the sit-in movement

The sit-ins at a lunch counter in Greensboro, North Carolina, in 1960 were significant to the civil rights campaign because they grew into a mass movement to challenge segregation in public places.

Events at Greensboro, 1960

- On 1 February 1960, four black students in North Carolina – David Richmond, Izell Blair, Franklin McCain and Joseph McNeil – waited to be served at a segregated lunch counter in the Woolworth department store.
- The students knew they would be asked to leave the 'whites only' area, but when told to do so by staff they refused to go. Instead, they held a 'sit-in', remaining in the store until closing time. Their aim was to generate publicity that would make Woolworth department stores end their policy of segregation.

> **Sit-in:** form of non-violent protest during which protesters refuse to leave a designated place or area.

- The following day, 25 more students arrived to join the Greensboro sit-in.
- By 4 February, there were more than 300 students, both black and white, working in shifts to continue the protest. After a week the sit-ins spread to other towns in North Carolina.
- Due to the loss of earnings and the continued disruption to business, in July the Greensboro Woolworth store desegregated. However, other Woolworth stores in the Southern states took longer: some did not desegregate until 1965, despite many more sit-in protests.

Organisation of the sit-ins

As the Greensboro sit-ins continued, CORE and the SCLC sent experienced campaigners to train students in non-violent protest methods.

On 15 April 1960, the Student Nonviolent Coordinating Committee (SNCC) was set up, in order to organise the kind of non-violent protests used previously by Martin Luther King and by CORE. SNCC trained students to cope with the hostility and harassment they faced during sit-ins and other demonstrations such as being sworn at, pushed and having drinks thrown over them.

> **Key principles of non-violent direct action**
> 👍 Demonstrate peacefully and visibly.
> 👍 Do not rise to provocation.
> 👍 Show your opponent up as a violent oppressor.

Demonstrators outside a Woolworth store in New York, on 13 February 1960, to protest against lunch counter discrimination.

White and black supporters: Some white Southerners joined CORE and SNCC. At first, the sit-ins were a protest organised by students, and mostly the students taking part were black. But by the end of 1960, campaigners were more mixed racially and no longer just students.

Media coverage: Positive news reports of the sit-ins resulted in support from black and white Americans in both the North and South. This led to demonstrations across the USA to challenge segregation in public spaces.

Significance of the Greensboro sit-ins

Visible to public: The sit-ins were a very visible form of public protest.

Spread quickly: Existing civil rights groups meant structures were already in place that helped the sit-ins to spread quickly.

Young people: Many young people thought that segregated lunch counters were wrong and humiliating, and were keen to protest against them.

Mass support: Large numbers of protesters (about 50 000 by autumn 1960) took part in the sit-ins.

Now try this

Write an acrostic poem using the name 'Greensboro' to sum up the events and significance of the protest at that time.

Remember, an acrostic poem is when the first letters of each line spell out a word or phrase.

Progress in civil rights, 1960–62

The years 1960–62 saw further examples of important progress for civil rights campaigners, who sought to speed up desegregation in public spaces and education.

Testing out Supreme Court rulings

- In 1956, the Supreme Court ruled that state transport must desegregate. However, bus station toilets and waiting rooms remained segregated, as these were not part of the ruling.
- In December 1960, the Supreme Court ordered desegregation of bus station facilities.
- In 1961, CORE activists organised bus journeys from the North to the Deep South, to test whether desegregation was really happening. CORE knew that segregation still existed, so its aim was to create negative media coverage of segregation so that the federal government would act to force states to desegregate.

Bus terminal in Tennessee showing a 'White Waiting Room' sign.

Timeline

The Freedom Riders, 1961

4 May Thirteen 'Freedom Riders, (a group of black and white Americans) started out from Washington, DC on two buses. The campaign organisers were CORE and the SCLC. Their aim was to show that desegregation of bus station facilities was not happening.

17 May SNCC organised ten Riders to bus from Nashville, Tennessee, to Birmingham, Alabama. No driver agreed to continue the journey, so the Riders stopped in Birmingham where a threatening crowd of segregationists confronted them.

24 May A police escort accompanied a new group of Freedom Riders travelling from Montgomery to Jackson, Mississippi. When they arrived in Jackson, the Riders were arrested and the federal government did not protect them.

1 Nov The federal government threatened to use federal officers to enforce desegregation if states continued to refuse to desegregate bus station facilities. The government wanted an end to the violence and the Freedom Rides. So Southern states began to desegregate bus facilities and the Freedom Rides were no longer needed.

15 May The first bus reached Anniston, Alabama and was attacked by over 100 KKK members. Someone threw a firebomb into the bus, but the passengers managed to escape before the bus exploded. Riders on the second bus were also attacked and beaten. In the end, all the Riders were rescued.

20 May Police escorted the Freedom Riders' bus to just outside Montgomery, Alabama, then left the Riders to defend themselves against a white mob at the bus station. They attacked and beat the Riders.

Summer Throughout the summer months there were 60 Freedom Rides. Over 300 Riders were jailed. Many were assaulted by police while in custody.

James Meredith, 1962

Meredith applied to the University of Mississippi after an earlier failed attempt to get a place there. The NAACP brought a successful court case, and the Supreme Court ordered the university to admit him. University officials ignored the Supreme Court's ruling and blocked Meredith from starting.

On 30 September, federal officials escorted Meredith on campus, where some 3000 segregationists attacked them. President Kennedy called for peace. Rioting broke out and many people were injured; some were killed. Federal troops were sent in to stop the rioting. Meredith finally registered on 1 October, but he continued to need armed guards while he completed his university studies.

Now try this

Write **one** paragraph to explain the progress made by civil rights activists, 1960–62.

Think about the campaign methods and the role of the federal authorities. (The information on page 8 about Greensboro would also be helpful when answering this question.)

Peaceful protests and their impact, 1963–65

By 1963, civil rights campaigners were seeking new ways to gain much-needed media attention, in order to put pressure on authorities in Southern states to improve the situation for black Americans there.

Events in Birmingham, 1963

Martin Luther King and the SCLC led the campaign in Birmingham, Alabama. Birmingham was chosen because:

- it was still completely segregated
- the local police chief – 'Bull' Connor – had a reputation as someone who could be provoked into violence
- black Americans had regularly been attacked there.

The Birmingham campaign included peaceful marches, sit-ins, boycotts and public meetings. Hundreds of arrests took place, including of young children. With the jails full, Connor ordered the use of water cannon and police dogs to deal with the protesters. This response to the peaceful protests was widely criticised and gained supportive news coverage for the civil rights campaign.

Police with dogs break up a civil rights demonstration in Birmingham, Alabama, 1963. Notice how the man is using a coat to protect his hand from possible dog bites. He does not appear to have seen the police officer with the raised truncheon.

The March on Washington, 1963

In August 1963, after events in Birmingham, Alabama, civil rights leaders, including Martin Luther King, organised a march of protesters from across the United States. The 'March on Washington' was for 'Jobs and Freedom'.

- More than 250 000 people took part in the march. Of these, about 40 000 were white Americans.
- The march was peaceful and was broadcast live on television around the world.
- King made his famous 'I have a dream' speech.

Aerial view of protesters at the March on Washington, 1963. At the time, this was the largest demonstration in US history.

Freedom Summer, 1964

In 1964 in Mississippi, SNCC and CORE set up the 'Freedom Summer'. A thousand volunteers went to Mississippi to help boost voter registration.

- Most volunteers were white college students from respectable families. Their social status would make any violence against them more newsworthy.
- They ran voter registration classes to teach black locals about passing the test to register to vote.
- 17 000 black Americans tried to register to vote; only 1600 were successful.
- In retaliation, the Ku Klux Klan burned crosses and set fire to black people's homes and churches.

Mississippi murders

On 21 June 1964, three activists, Michael Schwerner, Andrew Goodman (who were white) and James Chaney (who was black) were killed by a Klan lynch mob near Meridian, Mississippi. CORE and SNCC members tried to find the bodies of the murdered men. The bodies were eventually discovered and during the search the bodies of a further eight victims of the Klan were also discovered.

The 'Mississippi murders' showed the levels of hatred and violence Klan members used to stop civil rights.

Now try this

Give **two** impacts of each of the following: events in Birmingham, Alabama, 1963; the March on Washington, and the Mississippi Freedom Summer.

Civil rights law, 1964–65

In this period, important breakthroughs were made in passing new civil rights legislation in the USA.

Kennedy and Johnson and their contribution to civil rights laws

President John F. Kennedy, 1961–63

- Selected black people for high-level jobs, including Thurgood Marshall (who successfully argued the 1954 *Brown v. Topeka* case).
- Backed introduction of new civil rights laws after initially being reluctant to support civil rights. He became committed to the cause because of the impact of the civil rights protests and in particular the outrageous treatment of protesters at Birmingham.
- Sent federal troops to the University of Mississippi to protect James Meredith.
- Sent US marshals to escort the Freedom Riders and prevent them being attacked.

President Lyndon B. Johnson, 1963–69

- Continued to appoint black people to high-level jobs, including naming Patricia Harris as US Ambassador to Luxembourg in 1965.
- Urged Southern politicians to support 1964 Civil Rights Bill.
- Supported the 1964 Civil Rights Act and 1965 Voting Rights Act.
- Intervened to escort protesters marching from Selma to Montgomery in 1965.

President Kennedy was assassinated on 22 November 1963 in Dallas, Texas. Lyndon B. Johnson succeeded him as president.

The 1964 Civil Rights Act

- New powers forced school desegregation.
- Government could stop federal funding of state projects that promoted inequality.
- No discrimination in voter registration tests.
- Banned discrimination in public spaces and interstate businesses.
- Banned employment discrimination in larger businesses.
- Set up Equal Employment Opportunities Commission to combat work discrimination.

The 1965 Voting Rights Act

Johnson was heavily influenced by the Selma campaign, praising the courage of the activists and seeing the march as a turning point in the fight against racial prejudice and injustice.

- He introduced a standard voting registration process across the USA, controlled by federal government.
- States could introduce new voting rules only if the federal government agreed.
- Federal officials would take over voter registration in states where less than 50% of those qualified to vote failed to register.

The Selma to Montgomery marches, 1965

Early in 1965, the SCLC and King decided to campaign for voting rights in Selma, Alabama, to lend support to President Johnson's Voting Rights Act. Some campaigners held protests against voter registration tests while others tried to register to vote. Violence broke out with the police and a protester was killed.

On 7 March, 600 people set out to march 54 miles from Selma to Montgomery, Alabama, to publicise the right of black Americans to vote. State troops stopped the protesters outside Selma, using tear gas, clubs and cattle prods. The media reported the violence worldwide.

A second attempt to march from Selma to Montgomery, on 9 March, was unsuccessful. Following the march, a local white group murdered a white civil rights activist, causing public outrage. President Johnson now intervened, placing the Alabama state national guard under federal control and ordering it to give safe passage to the marchers. The third and final march took place on 21–24 March, with 25 000 protesters concluding the march from Selma to Montgomery on 25 March.

Now try this

Write **two** paragraphs describing the roles of Presidents Kennedy and Johnson in improving US civil rights in the 1960s.

Malcolm X

Malcolm X was a key figure in the fight for improved civil rights in the USA. He had a different philosophy from that of Martin Luther King and his views influenced Black Power.

For more about King's approach, go to page 5. Turn to page 13 to revise Black Power.

Malcolm X: his beliefs, methods and involvement with the Black Muslims

He had a troubled upbringing, during which white racists killed his father.

He was an effective public speaker and spoke with conviction and passion.

He thought non-violent direct action would never work, because white society would never consider black Americans as equals.

In a speech in June 1964, he said black people should defend themselves 'by any means necessary'. He criticised those who argued for non-violence; he said white Americans would never allow equality unless forced to do so.

Malcolm X

His birth name was Malcolm Little, which he later rejected as a slave name. He replaced 'Little' with 'X' for unknown.

He left the Nation of Islam in 1964, as he began to challenge NOI's ideas about Islam and race.

He was involved in crime and illegal drugs in his youth and went to prison, where he joined the **Nation of Islam** (NOI).

He became a spokesman for the Nation of Islam, arguing that black and white Americans should live separately. He believed white Americans could not help black Americans achieve equality.

He related well to angry young people in Northern US cities.

He set up the Organization of Afro-American Unity. It aimed to unite all people of African descent and achieve political and economic independence from white Americans.

Members of the Nation of Islam assassinated Malcolm X in 1965.

Before his death he came to believe integration with whites **might** be possible, as his pilgrimage to Mecca demonstrated that Muslims of different races could be united in their faith.

Nation of Islam, or Black Muslims: A radical group that mixed ideas from Islam with those of black separatism. They believed black Americans needed to create their own separate state, independently of white Americans.

Malcolm X's change of attitude

- Malcolm X left the Nation of Islam in 1964, to start up his own religious group – Muslim Mosque, Inc. (MMI).
- The Nation of Islam now became Malcolm X's enemy and started sending him death threats.
- Malcolm X went on a pilgrimage to Mecca in April 1964 and rejected many of his old beliefs about separatism.
- He decided to work with other civil rights groups and set up the Organization of Afro-American Unity (OAAU) in 1964.
- He met SNCC and CORE members to explore the possibility of working together to promote civil rights.

15 000 people attended Malcolm X's funeral on 27 February 1965.

The assassination of Malcolm X

Malcolm X's supporters kneel by him after he is shot 15 times by members of the Nation of Islam while speaking, on 21 February 1965 in Harlem. The Nation of Islam had previously firebombed Malcolm's home a number of times and he needed bodyguards.

Now try this

Create a flowchart to summarise Malcolm X's contribution to the civil rights movement.

Black Power, 1963–70

From 1963, some black civil rights groups rejected non-violent methods and instead turned to a more radical approach to civil rights, which they called 'Black Power'.

Why did Black Power emerge?

Rejected non-violence
- Results were too slow and did not have enough impact.
- Integration relied on black Americans fitting into a white society that had treated them very badly.

Ideas
- Influenced by the views of Malcolm X.
- **Demanded** change to improve the position of black Americans rather than **asking** for white Americans to change it.
- Believed that self-defence was justified.
- Wanted black Americans to feel self-respect and pride in their own heritage.

Campaigning
- Focused on wider social issues of poverty and unemployment.
- Got involved in wider campaigns like the anti-Vietnam War movement.

The Black Power salute was a raised clenched fist. It represented strength and intimidated those who were scared to talk about a violent revolution to achieve black equality in the USA. In October 1996, Stokely Carmichael defended the term 'Black Power', which his supporters chanted at demonstrations.

Significance of Stokely Carmichael

- After 1965, SNCC continued with the drive for voter registration. Yet many black Americans were dissatisfied that no political parties focused on black rights.
- Stokely Carmichael helped set up the Lowndes County Freedom Organization (LCFO) as a party to concentrate on issues most affecting black Americans. The party logo was a panther, and it became a symbol of black rights.
- In May 1966, Carmichael became Chairman of SNCC. He wanted a more radical approach to equality. More Black Power supporters joined SNCC and campaigned in the North, particularly in poor Northern ghettos.
- A 220-mile 'March against Fear' took place in Mississippi, in June 1966. On the second day, the walk's organiser, James Meredith, was shot and hospitalised, so King and Stokely Carmichael led it. King argued for non-violence but Carmichael's more radical speeches called for Black Power.

Significance of the 1968 Mexico Olympics

The 1968 Mexico Olympics provided an opportunity for black American athletes to show their support for Black Power. Tommie Smith and John Carlos won gold and bronze in the 200 metres. In the medals ceremony they raised their fists in the Black Power salute. They were widely criticised in the media and were banned from the team. However, many young black Americans admired them for taking this stand and making their political views clear in such a public way.

The Black Panthers

- Set up in 1966 by Huey Newton and Bobby Seale.
- Originally called 'The Black Panther Party for Self-Defense'.
- Believed black people needed black officials and black police to support the community.
- Prepared to work with white people holding the same beliefs.
- Had a radical 'ten-point plan' for transforming society, including the end of capitalism, free healthcare and the end of all wars.
- Uniform was a black beret, black trousers and black leather jacket.
- Carried guns for self-defence and tape recorders – to record police harassment.
- Set up breakfast clubs for poor black children, provided free shoes and medical services.

The Black Panthers were successful in providing black Americans living in poverty with financial help, but their ultimate goal of a radical social and economic revolution in the USA was not achieved.

Now try this

Draw and complete a table about Black Power. Include 'Ideas' in one column and 'Achievements' in another.

Remember, the term Black Power refers to a range of black American groups, including SNCC and the Black Panthers. Some groups were more radical than others.

The civil rights movement, 1965–75

There were successes and failures for the civil rights movement in the period from 1965–75. In 1968, King was assassinated and President Johnson published the Kerner Report into rioting.

The riots of 1964–67

- Between 1964 and 1968, there were 329 major riots in 257 Northern US cities.
- The riots began in New York City in July 1964, when a policeman shot a young black man. They were a reaction to ghetto conditions and violence during the Freedom Summer of 1964.
- There were riots in the Watts district of Los Angeles in August 1965. These were a response to police violence, ghetto conditions and the events in Selma that year.
- Riots followed every year in the summer months in different cities, mainly in the North, including Chicago and Cleveland in 1966, and Newark and Detroit in 1967.

Long-term causes: Black Americans lived unequal lives compared with white Americans. This led to anger and despair. They endured lower standards of education and discrimination from police and local officials.
Short-term causes: Specific incidents, such as a shooting, triggered each riot.

To read more about the Freedom Summer of 1964, turn to page 10. For more information on events in Selma during 1965, go to page 11.

The Kerner Report, 1968

Set up by Johnson in 1967, its findings were:
- the riots were the consequence of poor living conditions in the ghettos and the failure to respond to black complaints about them
- African Americans should be listened to and properly involved in resolving the problems
- policing methods must change because black communities do not trust the police
- policing during the riots made things worse
- money provided for improved living conditions and opportunities had not been spent on planned improvements, just on more police
- the media had exaggerated the riots.

King moves North

In 1966, King and the SCLC moved the focus of their campaigning to the North. Yet they struggled to connect with people in Northern cities. Their campaign began in Chicago, where they focused on fairer housing, but faced setbacks.

- The local mayor agreed to discussions and sounded reasonable, but did not act.
- Riots broke out and media coverage was negative. This did not help their cause.
- King's outspoken criticism of the USA's involvement in Vietnam meant the president was less supportive of him.

The assassination of Martin Luther King and its impact

King was shot and killed by James Earl Ray on his hotel balcony in Memphis, Tennessee, on 4 April 1968. There were violent responses to his murder across the USA, including rioting in Washington and Cleveland. James Earl Ray was given a long prison sentence. After the assassination:

The 1968 Civil Rights Act focused on fair housing and provided federal protection to civil rights workers.

Civil rights groups lost funding and membership – with civil rights laws, many white Americans saw the battle for civil rights as over.

Many white Americans related to King as a moderate. His death increased white opposition to black demands for equality.

Many black Americans became more radical after King's death, as they were increasingly impatient about the slow pace of change.

The funeral procession of Martin Luther King, in Atlanta, 9 April 1968. Over 100 000 mourners joined the procession.

Now try this

Write a description of King's campaign in the North. It should be no more than 200 words long.

Civil rights achievements up to 1975

By 1975 there had been significant progress in many areas of civil rights in the USA. However, in many ways racial equality remained a long way off.

Progress in US civil rights, 1969–74

Nixon's presidency saw the following changes for civil rights:

👍 Increased training for black people setting up businesses in black areas.

👍 Favourable tax terms to white-owned businesses that expanded into black areas.

👍 Job equality promoted by encouraging 'affirmative action' – the deliberate selection of a black person for a job.

👍 More black officials working in the White House.

👎 Nixon wanted black voters to vote for him, but balanced this against those white voters that he knew were still opposed to civil rights. He therefore portrayed improved civil rights to white voters as a means to control the black rioters, rather than arguing that it was their entitlement.

👎 Nixon has been criticised for patronising black Americans by presenting the promotion of black home ownership as a way to stop black Americans destroying property.

African Black Panther Party for civil rights meets at the Capitol, Washington, November 1975.

Examples of progress made:
• By 1970, 700 black elected officials were in office in the Southern states, a rise from only 25 in 1964.
• In 1973, Maynard Jackson was elected Atlanta's first African-American mayor.

What progress did the civil rights movement achieve by 1975?

Significant progress in **desegregation** was achieved, including in schools, transport and restaurants.

However, the campaigns to achieve **economic equality**, such as King's Poor People's Campaign and the campaigns of the Black Panthers, did not see a reduction in economic inequality. By the 1970s, the gap between the richest and poorest in the USA still depended on race. Black Americans still tended to have worse employment chances and were paid less for the work they did.

Turn to page 13 to find out more about the campaigns of the Black Panthers.

How did the federal government lead progress in civil rights, 1965–75?

In the early 1950s, the federal government and civil rights campaigners had hoped that enforced changes through the use of new laws would cause a change in attitude and that desegregation would spread quickly. However, by 1970, desegregation was not consistent and sometimes did not actually improve the situation for black Americans in real terms. For example, in some ways black schools had been better than integrated schools in terms of outcomes for black students.

Federal government continued to introduce new civil rights legislation. For example:
• the 1970 Voting Rights Act banned state literacy tests in all states
• the 1975 revision to the Voting Rights Act explicitly included other racial minorities.

Now try this

Draw up a table with two headings: 'Progress made in civil rights, 1965–75' and 'More progress needed'. Write down **three** examples under each of your headings.

US involvement in Vietnam, 1954–61

The US war in Vietnam was long and controversial. Conflict had been continuing between France and Vietnam since 1946. When the French finally withdrew in August 1954, the USA became heavily involved for a number of reasons.

Dien Bien Phu and French withdrawal

- After the end of the Second World War, France wanted to regain its former colony Vietnam.
- The Vietminh, led by Ho Chi Minh, wanted independence, and the Democratic Republic of Vietnam (DRV) was declared. The Vietminh had control of the north of Vietnam, while the French controlled the south. Fighting broke out between the two sides.
- In 1949, China became a communist country. China supported the Vietminh by giving supplies, advisers and troops.
- The USA began to send the French supplies, military advisers and soldiers. However, the soldiers were ordered not to actually fight because the USA was reluctant to get openly involved in the war.
- By 1954, US support was so strong it paid 80 per cent of the cost of France's war with the Vietminh.
- The French and the Vietminh fought a major battle at Dien Bien Phu in 1954. After 55 days of fighting the French were forced to surrender due to the strength of the Vietminh. This defeat was significant in leading the French to withdraw from Vietnam.
- The Geneva Conference (1954) attempted to restore peace. The Geneva Accords divided Vietnam into two countries along the 17th parallel, separated by a demilitarised zone where no soldiers were permitted.
- North Vietnam (the Democratic Republic of Vietnam) was led by Ho Chi Minh. South Vietnam (the State of Vietnam) was led by the US-backed ruler Bao Dai until 1955, when Ngo Dinh Diem became president.

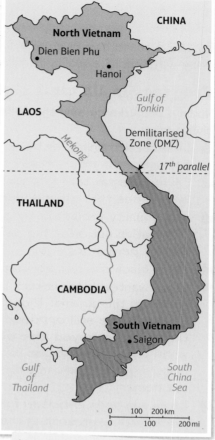

Vietnam and the neighbouring countries that were involved in the conflict.

Reasons for greater US involvement in Vietnam

1 Eisenhower and the 'domino theory'

The USA had a great fear about the spread of communism. Eisenhower was worried that if Vietnam became communist, other countries in the region would follow. This was called the 'domino theory'.

Eisenhower set up the Southeast Asia Treaty Organisation (SEATO) in September 1954. Its aim was to stop the spread of communism in Southeast Asia. SEATO included the USA, Britain, France and five other countries; they all agreed to act collectively to stop the spread of communism.

2 Weaknesses of Diem's government

Diem's unpopular government was corrupt, and it had little respect for the rural population and Buddhists (South Vietnam was mostly Buddhist, but Diem was Catholic).

Different revolutionary groups developed in South Vietnam to fight against Diem's government. They were collectively called the 'Vietcong' (or VC – short for 'Vietnamese Communists'). North Vietnam backed the VC and there was a civil war. Eisenhower supported Diem by sending advisers to train the South Vietnamese army (ARVN) to fight the VC. Eisenhower did not want to risk nuclear war with China and the USSR by sending US troops.

> ### Now try this
>
> Give **three** reasons why US involvement in Vietnam increased up to 1961.

Kennedy and Vietnam, 1961–63

Under President Kennedy (1961–63), there was greater US involvement in the conflict in Vietnam. Kennedy used a range of tactics to win the war but these had limited success.

Kennedy became US President in 1961. He agreed with the domino theory.

He wanted to avoid direct military action in Vietnam.

He recognised the Vietcong (VC) were gaining ground.

He sent more advisers to South Vietnam (around 16 000 more by late 1963).

President Kennedy, 1961–63

He authorised use of chemical sprays, such as Agent Orange, to kill crops and jungle areas the VC were hiding in from 1961 (Operation Ranch Hand).

He changed tactics to searching for VC fighters, not just trying to draw them into battle.

In 1961, Kennedy requested a report on the feasibility of sending in US soldiers for active service in Vietnam.

US concerns leading to Diem's overthrow

Kennedy had concerns about Diem's effectiveness as leader of South Vietnam.

- Kennedy believed that the VC were being beaten, but in January 1963, the ARVN lost the Battle of Ap Bac, even though it had US air support and five times as many soldiers as the VC.
- The US media reported the battle as a defeat, despite government attempts to present it positively; Kennedy worried about the negative publicity of Diem's leadership.
- On 6 May, Diem's government troops fired on a Buddhist procession, killing nine, which added to Diem's unpopularity among the Vietnamese people.
- On 11 June, a Buddhist monk burned himself to death (self-immolated) in protest about Diem's government. His protest generated worldwide publicity.
- Kennedy put pressure on Diem's government to make peace with the Buddhists, but Diem continued to persecute them.
- Kennedy did not want to publicly depose Diem, despite knowing how unpopular he was, but he made it obvious that he had withdrawn all support for his leadership. He now knew Diem's government would never be democratic.
- In November 1963, ARVN generals overthrew and assassinated Diem; the USA did not intervene to prevent this.

Kennedy felt the US government had a responsibility to help protect the new South Vietnam government from the spread of communism. He considered greater US military involvement in Vietnam, but wanted to help build a new democracy there. He wanted the new government to persuade the population to support its aims, rather than use repression.

The Strategic Hamlet Program, 1962

Diem and the USA built new villages to house locals away from the Vietcong, so the VC could not recruit them to fight. The aim was to provide security for the villagers and create support for the government. The hamlets were also supposed to have schools and medical centres.

The ARVN forcibly removed and relocated villagers. However, the villagers did not want to leave their ancestral homes. Also, there was not enough food or basic provisions in some of the new villages and many villagers starved to death. The program made Diem and the USA more unpopular in South Vietnam.

A fortified Vietnamese hamlet, 1963

Now try this

Describe **three** methods used by Kennedy to prevent the spread of communism in Vietnam.

Escalation of the conflict under Johnson

Under President Johnson (1963–69), the conflict in Vietnam escalated dramatically for a number of reasons. The Gulf of Tonkin incident in 1964 was central to increased US involvement in Vietnam.

Johnson becomes president, 1963

Johnson's aims	Johnson's problems
Stop the spread of communism.	The communists in Vietnam were getting stronger and harder to defeat.
Establish democratic government in South Vietnam supported by the people.	The government of South Vietnam was very weak and unpopular.
Ensure that the situation did not deteriorate into a nuclear war.	The USSR was a superpower with nuclear capability.

The Gulf of Tonkin incident, 1964

In August 1964, two US naval ships reported attacks by North Vietnamese torpedo boats off the North Vietnamese coast.

Causes	Consequences
• Increased build-up of US advisers in South Vietnam under Johnson. • Regular US patrols by ships, such as *Maddox* and *C. Turner Joy* in Gulf of Tonkin. • US involvement in ARVN raids on North Vietnam.	• Johnson ordered air strikes against North Vietnam. • Congress passed the Gulf of Tonkin Resolution, allowing Johnson to use armed force to defend South Vietnam and US troops already stationed there. • In response, the North Vietnamese expanded their involvement in South Vietnam.

Increasing threat of the Vietcong

- The Vietcong (VC) became more organised and effective, and their numbers increased.
- Some of the VC's ideas were popular among ordinary Vietnamese, who sympathised with their view of Americans as imperialists wanting to control Vietnam for their own ends.
- Many South Vietnamese were angry with the government for its dealings with the USA and policies such as the Strategic Hamlet Program.
- They received support from North Vietnam, which sent supplies and weapons to them (mostly provided by the USSR and China).
- Many rural South Vietnamese supported the VC. The increased support from civilians made the threat of the VC more extensive.

The Ho Chi Minh Trail

The North Vietnamese with China's help supported the VC in South Vietnam by sending troops and weapons via the Ho Chi Minh Trail.

The trail was a network of paths and smaller trails, which connected North and South Vietnam (often passing through Laos and Cambodia). It took about a month to get from one end to the other.

Over time the paths on the trail became wider and easier to use to send more support. By 1974, some parts of the trail were properly paved and dotted along the route there were underground hospitals, and fuel and weapons stores.

President Johnson signing the Gulf of Tonkin Resolution, 10 August 1964. This gave him power to escalate the war in Vietnam without consulting Congress following the Gulf of Tonkin incident. This meant that the lack of support for the war from Congress could be overcome.

While the Gulf of Tonkin Resolution stopped short of being an official declaration of war, it had the same outcome.

Remember that this is a summary: focus on the key points.

Now try this

Create a flowchart to sum up why the war in Vietnam escalated under President Johnson.

Conflict in Vietnam, 1964–68

The USA, the North Vietnamese and the Vietcong used very different tactics to try to secure victory.

Guerrilla tactics of the Vietcong

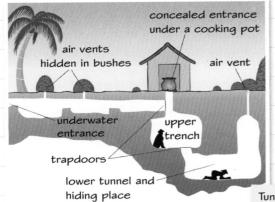

- air vents hidden in bushes
- concealed entrance under a cooking pot
- air vent
- underwater entrance
- upper trench
- trapdoors
- lower tunnel and hiding place

The Vietcong (VC) used a range of methods:
- planned ambushes
- set simple, but deadly traps
- did not wear military uniform so integrated with rural peasants
- stayed close to US deployments of soldiers so they couldn't be bombed easily
- sabotaged roads and bridges to make it difficult for the enemy to move around
- avoided open battles
- blended in with the local population so it was hard for members to be identified – could be male, female, young or old.

Tunnels allowed the VC to organise surprise attacks, store their supplies safely, hide securely and treat the wounded.

Operation Rolling Thunder

Early in 1965, there were still no US soldiers on the ground in Vietnam. Johnson wanted to force the North Vietnamese to negotiate a settlement so, in February 1965, the USA started a bombing campaign in North Vietnam called Operation Rolling Thunder.

Johnson resisted calls from the military to bomb extensively. So Rolling Thunder began gradually, near to South Vietnam. It targeted the Ho Chi Minh Trail, to stop supplies being taken south, and North Vietnam's small industrial base. Johnson avoided the capital Hanoi, the port Haiphong (where the USSR sent supplies into North Vietnam) and the border area with China, to avoid the war escalating and China and the USSR becoming more involved.

US tactic of 'search and destroy'

- Small groups of US soldiers tracked down VC camps then called in helicopters to spray chemicals on them and bomb them.
- The VC often left traps on the ground to kill or injure US soldiers.
- If any VC remained in the area, they used 'hit and run' attacks on US troops instead of fighting any battles.
- US troops destroyed any VC tunnels, weapons and supplies that they found.
- However, after US troops left the area, the VC returned. This sent out the message that US search and destroy methods were failing.
- The use of chemical sprays, and bombing of crops and homes made the USA unpopular with locals.

Tet Offensive, 1968

- Led by the North Vietnamese and VC in January–February 1968. Over 100 cities and US bases in South Vietnam were attacked.
- Initially, the North Vietnamese and VC drew US and ARVN troops away from cities and military bases by attacking the demilitarised zone.
- The North Vietnamese also suggested a negotiated settlement, which made the US think the communists were losing.
- On 30 January, North Vietnamese troops and the VC attacked high-profile places in Saigon, such as the US embassy, airport and radio station.
- The attack in Saigon was defeated, but US citizens were shocked at events.
- Eventually, US and ARVN troops recaptured the cities and bases that were attacked and the communists suffered very heavy losses (the VC were almost wiped out). However, the American public saw the Tet Offensive as a terrible failure.

Chemical weapons

The US sprayed large areas of Vietnam with chemicals, such as napalm, to destroy jungle and crops. The chemicals caused birth defects and widespread starvation.

Now try this

List the different tactics used by the Vietcong. Describe **one** positive or negative effect of each.

19

Changes under Nixon, 1969–73

President Nixon worked on several different approaches to get the USA out of Vietnam. However he still wanted to ensure that South Vietnam did not become a communist-led country.

The Nixon Doctrine

On 25 July 1969, President Nixon put forward his ideas about Vietnam, Southeast Asia and the USA – known as the Nixon Doctrine.

- The USA would follow through on any existing support it had promised its allies and help them against nuclear attacks.
- However, from now on the United States would only provide financial help and training against threats from countries that did not have nuclear capacity – it would not provide soldiers.

In the USA, public opinions differed about Vietnamisation. Some supported the aims of the war and wanted to continue with active involvement. Others wanted American withdrawal as soon as possible.

Key features of Vietnamisation

Putting the ideas behind the Nixon Doctrine into practice was called Vietnamisation.

- Nixon wanted US troops to withdraw from Vietnam, while also giving the appearance the USA had not lost the war.
- The South Vietnamese army (ARVN) was to take over more of the actual fighting, thus reducing the number of US military deaths.
- The US government's focus was now to send money and advisers, not soldiers.
- The US government's aim was to ensure South Vietnam remained an independent, non-communist country – in this way the USA would not lose face over the outcomes in Vietnam.

Vietnamisation failed because US training and equipment was not enough to ensure the ARVN was ready to take over the fighting. The ARVN also suffered from corruption and desertion.

US troops withdraw from Vietnam

Most Americans wanted US troops to come home. Troops began to be withdrawn from 1968 onwards. Once soldiers knew they would soon be leaving, their desire to fight was severely reduced. Many tried to avoid battle and some killed their officers to stop them leading them into situations where their lives were at risk. Drug use also rocketed among US troops.

Attacks on Cambodia, 1970, and Laos, 1971

In 1970, despite creating public hostility, Nixon sent US troops to Cambodia to stop the North Vietnamese from helping Cambodia's communists to power there. Congress was outraged and cancelled the 1964 Gulf of Tonkin Resolution. Congress also reduced money for war and demanded faster troop reductions from Vietnam.

Turn to page 18 for more information on the Gulf of Tonkin incident and resolution of 1964.

In 1971, the USA gave air support for a South Vietnamese invasion of Laos, to stop the spread of communism there. There was bloody fighting between North and South Vietnamese soldiers in Laos. The South Vietnamese did not fight well, increasing doubts about their ability to hold back communism in South Vietnam after US troops went home.

Bombing of North Vietnam, 1972

- In April 1972, the USA bombed North Vietnam in heavy air raids to weaken it.
- All areas were targeted and mines were dropped into Haiphong harbour to stop supplies from China and the USSR coming by sea.
- Radio and communications were destroyed.
- The North Vietnamese war industry was severely damaged.
- The bombing led to calls from the USSR and China for North Vietnam to sign a peace deal.

Go to page 24 for details of the peace deal.

Now try this

Summarise key information about Nixon's approach in Vietnam from 1969 to 1972 on a timeline.

Reasons for the growth of opposition

A range of factors, especially the student movement and media coverage of what was happening in Vietnam, led to a growth in anti-war feeling.

The student movement

Initial approval for the war declined as US involvement escalated over time. The period saw a growth in student anti-war organisations.

Many young people rejected the attitudes of previous generations and wanted social change.

A new 'counter culture' was emerging and students were a central part of it.

Anti-war demonstration in New York, 1967, outside the United Nations building.

Many students were opposed to the draft.

Student numbers increased to 8.5 million in 1970 from about 6 million five years earlier.

In 1967, ex-soldiers formed Vietnam Veterans Against the War. They held protests and some publicly threw away their medals.

TV and media coverage of the war

Unlike earlier wars, Vietnam was the first conflict where reporters were able to travel with the troops into the war zone and report back on what they saw. This brought the Vietnam War into people's homes via television; indeed, the Vietnam conflict has been described as a 'media war' because media coverage was so important to public perceptions of the conflict. The media also reported on the large-scale anti-war protests that were spreading across the USA.

You need to be able to explain **why** media coverage of the war had an impact on public opinion of the Vietnam conflict.

Impact of media images and footage on opinion at home

Many Americans started to believe the TV reporters were being more honest than the politicians about what was really going on in Vietnam. The news reports inspired the American public to get involved in understanding and debating the issues. There was a growing feeling that the government could not be trusted to keep the public properly informed about what was happening. Many Americans also felt the government was misrepresenting how the war was progressing.

Vietnam and the draft system

- The draft forced men aged 18–25 years to serve in the military forces. Men who were chosen for military service were sent draft cards telling them where to report for duty.

- In 1966, the first men were drafted; they were chosen on the grounds that the US authorities viewed them as 'delinquent', i.e. they did not behave in socially acceptable ways, for example being involved in petty crime. Next, volunteers were used. Finally, men aged 18 to 25 years were called up.

- In 1969, a lottery system replaced the old process for the draft. Men born between 1944 and 1950 were issued a number and called up at random.

- Of the 2.6 million US soldiers who served in Vietnam, 650 000 were draftees.

The impact of increased conscription

The draft system led to widespread public criticism about unfairness, especially as the poorest were hardest hit. Some men burned their draft card or refused to join up. This was a criminal offence so 'draft dodgers' had to go into hiding to avoid arrest. Some fled to Canada. Men from wealthier families avoided or postponed being called up by going to college or by studying abroad.

A man burns his draft card at an anti-draft demonstration in Washington D.C., 1970.

Now try this

List **five** reasons why the anti-war movement grew in the USA, especially among young people.

Continued opposition to the war

The My Lai massacre of 1968 and the Kent State University shootings in 1970 led to massive public outcry about the Vietnam War.

My Lai Massacre, 1968

On 16 March 1968, US troops were sent to the village of My Lai in South Vietnam, where they were told they would come under Vietcong fire. They found only women, children and old men in the village. They killed everyone they found (at least 347, and possibly over 500, civilians) as well as their animals. After stopping to eat lunch, they returned to base.

Sergeant Ron Haeberle, a war photographer, accompanied the soldiers and took photos of what happened.

Women and children in My Lai, March 1968, just before US soldiers shot them dead.

Public reaction to the massacre

People in the USA were not sure what to believe about what had taken place. The government was accused of withholding information. Photos of the massacre were released to CBS News in December and the public saw this as evidence of a serious cover-up. The US public was horrified.

Trial of Lt Calley

Lt Calley led the military action at My Lai on the day of the massacre. He claimed that he had been acting on direct orders from his seniors when the massacre was carried out.

The Peers Enquiry later found that Calley was indeed following orders and that high-level army officials, including generals, were involved in the cover-up.

Lt Calley was found guilty of 22 murders and sentenced to life imprisonment – although his sentence was later reduced to three years. Controversially, even though 18 further officers had charges brought against them, no other soldier faced trial.

Timeline

Kent State University shootings, 1970

2 May There were several demonstrations and a military training building on campus was set ablaze.

4 May Officials stopped a planned demonstration but 2000 people protested anyway. Tear gas did not break up the crowd and they hurled empty canisters and debris at the National Guardsmen. The National Guard opened fire on the students, killing four and injuring nine.

1 May In Ohio, a group of Kent State University students buried a copy of the US Constitution in protest at Nixon's decision to send US troops into Cambodia.

3 May The numbers of protesters swelled to over 1000 and the mayor declared an emergency. 900 members of the National Guard were called out, armed with rifles and tear gas. Tear gas was used to disperse several demonstrations.

Significance of the Kent State University shootings

- Photos of the shootings of the students were published across the USA and the world.
- The public was shocked and outraged in the USA and worldwide by what had happened.
- The white middle-class students were unarmed and two of the dead students had been simply bystanders, not even involved in the protests.

Remember to include different causes when explaining why.

Now try this

Write **one** paragraph to explain why there was an increase in opposition to the Vietnam War.

Support for the Vietnam War

Many different groups in the United States supported the Vietnam War, despite the opposition and negative media coverage that the war generated. Different Americans had a range of reasons for believing the war in Vietnam had to be fought and won.

Fear of communism

- The Cold War made Americans paranoid about the 'communist threat'.

- By 1954, the fear of communism spreading to other countries was still very strong, although domestically the fear of communism had lessened.

> Eisenhower argued that to lose in Vietnam would inevitably lead to a far-reaching spread of communism in the region. He maintained that countries in Southeast Asia were under threat as well as ultimately Japan and Australia.

- Eisenhower first used the phrase 'falling domino' at a news conference in 1954, to express his concerns about the spread of communism.

- President Kennedy, in his inaugural (first) speech as president, argued that US security would be undermined as result of the domino effect.

To find out more about the domino effect, turn to page 16.

> 'Hard hats': the nickname for construction workers who actively supported the Vietnam War. At a protest in May 1970, a group wearing hard hats beat up anti-war protesters. The police made little attempt to protect the anti-war demonstrators.

Patriotism

Many Americans were concerned to keep the USA's standing in the world as high as possible. They did not want a defeat in Vietnam to lead to their country 'losing face'. Some Americans were very patriotic and saw it as their utmost duty to accept the authority of the government and to do their part in supporting their country, whatever the cost to them. They believed that fighting communism in Vietnam was their patriotic obligation. Many working-class people broadly supported the aims of the war.

Pro-war protesters at a demonstration in support of escalating the Vietnam War further.

Nixon sitting among stacks of supportive telegrams sent to the White House after his 'silent majority' speech on 3 November 1969.

The silent majority

In a televised speech on 3 November 1969, Nixon argued that 'the great silent majority' of Americans supported his Vietnam policy. He was right. A survey showed 77 per cent of Americans backed his plans for the Vietnam War and this support meant:

- that Congress passed resolutions approving Nixon's approach in Vietnam

- Nixon could show North Vietnam that he had strong support, helping him to persuade them to reach a settlement

- Nixon could hold out for an exit from Vietnam that, in theory, allowed the USA to withdraw with 'honour'.

Now try this

Imagine you are a supporter of the war in Vietnam. Write a telegram of no more than 100 words to President Nixon, explaining the reasons for your support.

The peace process and end of war

The process of reaching an end to the war involved an extended period of talks between the USA, North Vietnam and South Vietnam. Talks began in Paris in 1968.

Reasons for the peace negotiations up to 1972

USA's reasons	Shared reasons	North Vietnam's reasons
• Victory in Vietnam no longer seemed possible, especially after the problems with the Tet Offensive • Growing opposition to the war • Congress was reluctant to finance the continuation of the war • Nixon was keen to appear the peacemaker in Vietnam for political gain at home	• High numbers of dead and wounded • Costs of the war • The war could drag on for years to come	• China and the USSR wanted North Vietnam to make peace and might withdraw help • North Vietnam was being bombed heavily

Turn to page 19 to find out more about the Tet Offensive of 1968.

Features of the negotiations, 1973

- After negotiations had broken down in 1972, further talks began in Paris on 8 January 1973.
- All parts of the peace agreement were to be supervised by an international body.
- The USA would pay for reconstruction across Vietnam.

The North Vietnamese and South Vietnamese thought the war had not actually ended, seeing 'the peace' as temporary while the Americans withdrew.

The Paris Peace Agreement, 1973

The Paris Peace Agreement, signed by the USA, North Vietnam, South Vietnam and the Provisional Revolutionary Government of Vietnam on 27 January 1973, brought an end to the war and peace to Vietnam.

How was it significant?

The Paris Peace Agreement gave the USA an opportunity to withdraw from Vietnam. Yet in the long run it failed to secure the future of an independent non-communist South Vietnam. South Vietnam's economy crashed due to bad harvests, and a large reduction in US aid and investment. This contributed to the unpopularity of the new South Vietnamese government, and the Vietcong were soon popular in the village communities once more.

North Vietnam continued to seek a united, communist Vietnam and became impatient with the refusal of the President of South Vietnam, President Thieu, to talk. They resumed combat with South Vietnam in late 1974. The ARVN could not fend off the attack but Congress would not approve funds for the USA to intervene. The South Vietnamese capital, Saigon, fell in April 1975.

Key agreements

- All countries would accept Vietnam as a single reunified country through independent negotiation (with no outside interference).
- There would be an immediate ceasefire.
- US troops, equipment and advisers would be withdrawn and military bases removed.
- There would be no US government intervention in Vietnamese politics or militarily.
- The government of a new unified Vietnam would be chosen in fair and independent elections.

The economic and human costs of the Vietnam War for the USA

- The war cost the US economy $167 billion. The expense led to cutbacks in federal spending on domestic issues and caused economic problems.
- Over 58 000 US soldiers died; 75 000 were left with a serious permanent disability; 850 000 suffered severe mental health problems, including post-traumatic stress. There was a high rate of suicide among veterans of the war.

After the fall of Saigon in 1975, North and South Vietnam merged on 2 July 1976 to form the Socialist Republic of Vietnam.

Now try this

List **three** consequences of the Paris Peace Agreement, 1973.

The strengths of North Vietnam

US failure in the war can be explained by understanding the range of advantages – cultural, political and geographical – the North Vietnamese had. The USA found these difficult to match.

Strengths of North Vietnam

👍 Vietnam had previously been one country so the North had a good geographical and cultural understanding of the South.

👍 Many people in North and South Vietnam wanted to be reunited as a single country.

👍 The North Vietnamese, unlike the Americans, had a good knowledge of the natural environment in South Vietnam.

👍 They shared a language with the South Vietnamese.

👍 The North Vietnamese expected full commitment to the war from the oldest to the youngest citizen.

👍 Children were given military training and performed support roles, like carrying messages.

👍 The North Vietnamese believed that fighting and dying for their country was a matter of honour.

👍 Opposing the aim of the war – to reunify their country with the South Vietnamese people – was not an option in North Vietnamese political culture. Open political opposition to the government was not allowed.

A US marine carries a Vietnamese woman who was suspected of being a Vietcong. She is blindfolded.

Significance of Soviet and Chinese support

North Vietnam had financial help from other communist countries – China and the USSR. They sent over $3 billion in aid to North Vietnam between 1954 and 1967.

Soviet support: From 1965, after the US military escalation took hold, the USSR became North Vietnam's main source of economic aid.

Chinese support: From the start of the war against the French, China gave technical military and financial help to North Vietnam. After the 1964 Gulf of Tonkin incident, which marked a turning point for US involvement in Vietnam, the Chinese dramatically increased their support for North Vietnam and the Vietcong in South Vietnam. Between 1965 and 1971, over 320 000 Chinese troops were sent to North Vietnam.

Vietcong tactics and commitment

The guerrilla tactics of North Vietnam's allies, the Vietcong (VC), were difficult to undermine. The VC were used to fighting in jungle conditions and were well organised and equipped for guerrilla-style warfare.

The strong commitment of the VC and North Vietnamese troops was also difficult to challenge, as they had a clear ideology about why they needed to win the war and the reasons they were fighting. In comparison, the ARVN received poor training and did not have the same levels of belief in what they were fighting for.

Turn to page 19 for more on guerrilla warfare.

How did the Ho Chi Minh Trail help North Vietnam win the war?

Laos and Cambodia allowed the Ho Chi Minh Trail to operate in their countries. This was a vital supply route for the North Vietnamese to reach the VC in South Vietnam. Militarily it caused the USA a lot of difficulty. It was about 1000 km long and some sections of it were made-up trails to trick the enemy. Thousands of Vietnamese were involved in keeping the route open and workable. The Americans used biological weapons to deforest the jungle and expose the trail, yet despite this the route was kept going throughout the war.

Now try this

To read more on the Ho Chi Minh Trail, turn to page 18.

Complete a table to summarise the different types of advantages the North Vietnamese had. Head the columns 'Political advantages', 'Geographical advantages' and 'Cultural advantages'.

The weaknesses of US armed forces

The Americans lacked an understanding of the Vietnamese culture, geographical environment and political landscape, which made it difficult for them to win in Vietnam despite their military strength.

Lack of knowledge and awareness

1. Vietnam was very 'alien' to most Americans, who did not understand anything about the country they were at war with. US soldiers found the war more difficult as a result.

2. Many Americans underestimated their enemy and held ignorant and racist views about their inferiority as an opponent.

3. US military leaders and strategists did not try to understand the conflict from the viewpoint of the Vietnamese people and this put them at a real disadvantage.

The geographical distance between the USA and Vietnam is over 13 500 km.

Political and economic weaknesses

- For the first time, the USA fought a war for which there was no clear public agreement about whether the conflict was justified.

- Also for the first time in US history, war veterans wanted the war to stop and even handed in their medals in protest.

- There was a lot of media criticism about the war aims and the methods used.

- The US government ignored public opposition to the war but ultimately had to listen to the anti-war movement, as presidents and members of Congress relied on public support to be elected.

- When Congress restricted funding of the war after 1971 there were shortages of equipment for US troops.

Failure of US tactics

The US army benefited from superior military technology, including helicopters and advanced weaponry. However, in this context it did not help the US military to secure a victory. The USA:

- failed in its tactics, mistakenly believing that victory could be won by deploying more troops and ordering more bombing of North Vietnam

- over-estimated its successes, basing calculations on how many villages they destroyed or Vietcong they killed rather than how much territory they controlled.

Failure to win Vietnamese hearts and minds

While propaganda claimed the USA wanted democracy for South Vietnam, the South Vietnamese saw the USA as simply a foreign power interfering in their country. So the US-backed South Vietnamese government was very unpopular. It was also hated for its ties to French colonial interests of the past that were seen as anti-Vietnamese.

Many local people in South Vietnam had far more sympathy with the ideas and values of the Vietcong and North Vietnam than with a government imposed on them by the USA.

US troops were young and inexperienced and lacked relevant training in guerrilla warfare. The failures bred low morale. This in turn led to fragging (the intentional killing of officers by troops) and drug abuse. Many soldiers used alcohol and marijuana. When the US army clamped down on this, soldiers turned to other drugs, including heroin.

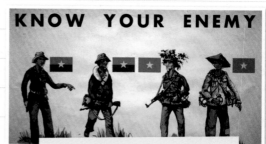

US chart for training soldiers, to help them understand the enemy.

Now try this

Write **one** paragraph to explain the main weaknesses of the USA in fighting the Vietcong.

Impact of US opposition to the war

The Vietnam War affected the USA in a number of ways: in terms of the lives lost and destroyed, the financial cost of the war and how American society was changed by the experience.

Impact of war opposition: a deeply divided society

1. The war led to a growing gulf between the public and previously trusted institutions, such as the government and armed services.

2. Returning soldiers were sometimes met with real hostility. As the anti-war movement grew, veterans could be targeted as 'baby killers'. Sometimes they were verbally or physically attacked. Some veterans found it difficult to find work.

3. There was a high suicide rate among returning soldiers. After the Second World War, veterans were treated as heroes, yet men returning from Vietnam were sometimes outcasts who felt that US society had let them down. They had been made to fight a war that US society, as a whole, did not support, and they carried the responsibility and guilt for this.

Vietnam War veterans, wearing 'Vets for Peace in Vietnam' hats, march to Washington, D.C., 1969, as part of a 600 000-strong demonstration. Many veterans joined the anti-war movement because they were disillusioned with the war's aims and methods.

Turn to pages 21–22 for more on the reasons behind opposition to the Vietnam War in the USA.

Financial impact

As well as the war expenditure, US society was affected by the lack of resources to address the problems they had domestically. For example, Johnson's 'Great Society' agenda, which aimed to reduce inequality and racial divisions, lost money that was spent on the war instead.

For more on President Johnson's attempts to reduce inequality and racial divisions, turn to page 11.

Pressure on US government of anti-war movement

- The reputation of the USA was diminished as a result of the war in Vietnam.

- The US government was concerned that involvement abroad should not lead to similar problems to those encountered in Vietnam.

- By the end of 1975, the whole of Vietnam was under a communist government, so the war seemed to have been pointless.

- In the 1950s, the American public had respect for its government but 20 years later the general feeling was that people should be more questioning of the power of, and decisions made by, government. The Vietnam War played a big part in this shift in attitude towards the government.

Anti-war protest outside the city hall in San Francisco, 1973.

Now try this

List **three** ways in which US society was affected by opposition to the Vietnam War.

Exam overview

This page introduces you to the main features and requirements of the Paper 3 Option 33 exam paper.

About Paper 3

- Paper 3 is for your modern depth study.
- The USA, 1954–75: conflict at home and abroad is a modern depth study and is Option 33.
- It is divided into two sections: Section A and Section B. You must answer **all** questions in both sections.
- You will receive two documents: a question paper, in which you also write your answers, and a Sources/Interpretations Booklet, which you will need for Section B.

 The Paper 3 exam lasts for 1 hour 20 minutes (80 minutes). There are 52 marks in total. You should spend about 25 minutes on Section A and about 55 minutes on Section B.

Links You can see examples of all six questions on pages 29–36 and in the practice questions on pages 37–50.

The questions

The questions for Paper 3 will always follow this pattern:

Section A: Question 1

Give **two** things you can infer from Source A about…   **(4 marks)**

Complete the table.

Question 1 targets Assessment Objective 3 (analysing, evaluating and using sources to make substantiated judgements). Spend about 5 minutes on this question, which focuses on **inference** and **analysing** sources. Look out for the key term 'infer'.

Section A: Question 2

Explain why…   **(12 marks)**

Two prompts and your own information.

Question 2 targets both AO1 (showing knowledge and understanding of the topic) and AO2 (explaining and analysing historical events using historical concepts such as causation, consequence, change, continuity, similarity and difference). Spend about 18 minutes on this question.

Section B: Question 3(a)

How useful are Sources B and C for an enquiry into…?   **(8 marks)**

Use the sources and your knowledge of the historical context.

Question 3(a) also targets AO3. Spend about 12 minutes on this question, which is about **evaluating the usefulness** of contemporary sources.

Section B: Question 3(b)

Study Interpretations 1 and 2…

What is the main difference between these views?   **(4 marks)**

Use details from both interpretations.

Questions 3(b) and 3(c) target AO4 (analysing, evaluating and making judgements about interpretations). Spend about 5 minutes on each of these questions, which are about **suggesting and explaining** why the interpretations differ.

Section B: Question 3(c)

Suggest **one** reason why Interpretations 1 and 2 give different views about…   **(4 marks)**

You can use sources provided to help explain your answer.

Section B: Question 3(d)

How far do you agree with Interpretation 1/2 about…?

(16 marks + 4 marks for SPaG and use of specialist terminology)

Use both interpretations and your knowledge of the historical context.

Question 3(d) also targets AO4. Spend approximately 30 minutes on this question, which is about **evaluating** an interpretation. Up to 4 marks are available for **spelling, punctuation, grammar (SPaG)** and use of **specialist terminology**.

Sources and interpretations

This exam asks you to analyse and evaluate both sources and interpretations, and you need different skills for each.

Questions 1 and 3(a)

Here you will be asked to look at sources. These sources could be posters, accounts from people at that time, photographs or any written or visual source that is **from the period**. As the sources are generated from that time it is helpful to think about the nature of the source, the origin, who produced it, and the purpose for which it was produced.

Questions 3(b), (c) and (d)

Here you will be asked to read interpretations of a particular enquiry or event from two different historians. Unlike analysing sources, interpretations are written **after the time period or event**. They are often written by historians or commentators who express their views and opinions about historical people, events and changes. As they are people's views and judgements based on evidence there can be differences, and sometimes clear disagreements, about what people think.

Content: what information can you get directly from the source and its caption? It is important to spend time reading and studying sources before you read the exam questions.

Bias: a source is still useful even if you think it is biased – it can be good for assessing people's opinions of an event, for example.

Nature: what type of source is it – a diary entry, newspaper article, cartoon? This will help you to assess reliability, usefulness and purpose.

Language: in written sources, the author's language should give you clues about whether they are biased or even unreliable. Using appropriate examples by quoting directly from the source will help you gain better marks. Language can also tell you about the purpose of a source.

Hints and tips for examining sources

Origins: the caption should tell you who produced the source and when. The origin will help you assess its reliability, usefulness and purpose.

Purpose: the reason a source was created could be one of the questions by itself, but this will also help you to assess its reliability and usefulness.

Selection: what has the author/artist chosen to include? What have they chosen to leave out? It's important to consider both of these when you are thinking about the reliability, usefulness and purpose of a source.

Hints and tips for analysing and evaluating interpretations

How complete?	How objective?	What is the chosen emphasis?
The interpretations can be different because they are concerned with finding out about different aspects of the enquiry and may cover different ground. Sometimes, historians set out to look at one aspect specifically, whereas others may want to look at related issues in a broader sense.	Historians can hold different views because they come from a particular school of thought. Therefore, their questions and answers are shaped by their wider views of society and how it works and has worked in the past. This can have an important impact on the judgements and opinions they hold about historical matters.	Sometimes, historians use the same sources but reach different views because they place a different level of importance on the same evidence. They may have access to the same material sources as each other, but will draw different conclusions about the significance of that evidence.

Question 1: Making inferences

Question 1 on your exam paper will ask you to 'infer from Source A...'. There are 4 marks available for this question.

Source A: South Carolina, 1957: a man stands outside his shop with 'WHITE ONLY' signs either side of him.

Making inferences from a source

Making inferences means working something out that is not shown directly. First of all, think about what is suggested or implied by the source and then try to show how the source helped you make that inference. Include supporting details from the source to back up what you say.

Worked example

Give **two** things you can infer from Source A about segregation laws in the USA in the 1950s.

Complete the table below to explain your answer.

(4 marks)

 **Links** You can revise the Southern states' segregation laws on page 1.

Sample answer

(i) What I can infer:

The segregation laws affected ordinary everyday life for black and white Americans, who even shopped for groceries in different stores.

Details in the source that tell me this:

The signs are clearly marked 'white only', to make sure that black Americans know they are not welcome in that store.

(ii) What I can infer:

Segregation was legally permitted in South Carolina in 1957.

Details in the source that tell me this:

The caption gives the date and location of the photograph. The shop owner or worker is photographed right next to the signs, as though he is either proud of his segregated shop or so used to segregation that he doesn't think anything about being pictured by the 'white only' signs.

The exam paper will give you a structure like this for your answer.

How to make inferences: Sometimes it is helpful to think about what you can see and then move on to think about what it **suggests**. You need to make sure that you don't just describe the source but go further and show you can infer information.

It is useful to think carefully about the caption describing the source, including any dates given. The context of **when** a source was produced will help you to **analyse** the source, rather than just describe it.

Remember that for some photographic sources, it can be important to consider their intended **audience** and **purpose**.

Question 2: Explaining causes

Question 2 on your exam paper will ask you to 'Explain why...'. There are 12 marks available for this question.

Worked example

Explain why there was growing US opposition to the Vietnam War by the mid 1960s.

You may use the following in your answer:

- there were 420 000 US troops in Vietnam in July 1967
- My Lai massacre

You **must** also use information of your own. **(12 marks)**

Explaining key features and causes

Explaining why involves looking at the key features of something and thinking about its causes. Key features are accurate and relevant knowledge. Causes are what led to a situation or change happening. To explain causes, you must show how a number of causes led to that event or change.

You must use your own knowledge and not limit yourself to the bullet points.

🎧 **Links** You can revise opposition to the Vietnam War on pages 21 and 22.

Sample extract

Some people in the USA were worried about the increased number of soldiers sent to Vietnam and the rising death toll. By 1967 the number of soldiers fighting there was over 400 000.

The media reported what was going on and this made some Americans unhappy about what was happening in Vietnam.

Here the student has given a correct cause but only a vague answer, and hasn't developed an explanation.

This is also a correct cause and the beginning of an explanation: the student needs to add more detail to the explanation to improve this answer.

Improved extract

Increased opposition was partly driven by attacks against civilians during the Vietnam War. In 1968 a company of American soldiers attacked villagers in My Lai, where around 500 people, including vulnerable women, old people and children, were savagely killed. It became known as the My Lai massacre. The army organised a cover-up of what had taken place, until one of the soldiers revealed the truth. Even after the crimes were investigated, only one soldier was actually convicted of a role in the murders. This all added to opposition, as not only were some people in the USA concerned about the Vietnamese death toll, they were increasingly angry about the behaviour of the US army and those in charge and the shocking brutality of the war.

Another important cause of increased US opposition to the war was the coverage offered by the US and world media, as TV was watched by an increasing number of Americans. The coverage of the Vietnam War was extensive and allowed the effects of the war to be brought into their living rooms. Images, including Malcolm Browne's photo of a Vietnamese Mahayana Buddhist monk setting himself on fire in 1963, had a deep impact on many Americans and made them question the war. When demands were made for increased troop numbers to be sent to fight, it raised further concerns with the American public about whether they wanted their sons, husbands and brothers to be fighting in the war.

Identify the reasons that led to increased US opposition to the war.

State the cause and explain why it led to more opposition.

🎧 **Links** The information about the cover-up shows use of relevant knowledge. Revise these events on page 22.

Use your knowledge of the period to support your answer with specific examples.

Using 'Another important cause... was' to introduce a new point is a good way of writing a clear answer.

Question 3(a): Evaluating usefulness

Question 3(a) on your exam paper will ask you to evaluate 'How useful are Sources B and C...'. There are 8 marks available for this question.

Worked example

Study Sources B and C on page 36.

How useful are Sources B and C for an enquiry into the success of the Montgomery Bus Boycott?

Explain your answer, using Sources B and C and your knowledge of the historical context.   **(8 marks)**

 Links   You can revise the Montgomery Bus Boycott on pages 4 and 5.

Judging usefulness of sources

To judge the usefulness of a source, you need to think about the enquiry question and the criteria you will use to reach your decision. You will need to consider the **provenance** of each source – its nature, origin and purpose, and whether these make the source useful or not in addressing the enquiry question.

Sample extract

The leaflet is written by racists and handed out in Montgomery during the time of the boycott. It is very extreme and says the negro race should be abolished using 'guns, bows and arrows, sling shots and knives'. It says those involved in the boycott have to be stopped or they will get more powerful and they will 'wake up to find Rev. King in the White House'.

Source B is useful because it shows the extreme hatred that the black people in Montgomery had to face. It shows that racists hated the black Americans for getting organised and campaigning.

 This answer lacks analysis and describes rather than judges the usefulness of the sources.

Key terms
Provenance: the origin of a source.

Nature: what type of source it is, such as a propaganda poster or a speech extract.

Purpose: the reason a source was created.

Improved extract

Both sources are useful for this enquiry but in different ways. Source B is a WCC leaflet distributed during the bus boycott. It reveals the deep hatred and violence that black Americans living in Montgomery suffered at the hands of white racists, who called them 'black devils'. It is useful because it shows that the protesters were so determined that they persisted despite these attitudes. It also shows that their non-violent methods, boycotting the buses and walking to work, were perceived as a real threat to the status quo. That is why the writer of the leaflet predicts they need to be stopped or they will gain real political power and end up 'in the White House' one day.

The Rosa Parks photograph in Source C shows her at the front of a city bus the day after integrated buses were introduced in Montgomery. The photograph must have been taken to be used for publicity purposes, to show the end result of the successful boycott campaign. It's useful for this enquiry, as it suggests that Parks had a central role in the boycott. However, the drawbacks are that it doesn't help us to understand how her actions were linked to other individuals and organisations in the campaign and could lead some people to overemphasise her contribution to the success of the boycott.

 You should use criteria about origins and audience in judging the usefulness of the source for the enquiry.

Use specific terms to show you understand and are addressing the task, such as: 'reveals', 'suggests', 'shows', 'drawbacks', 'because'.

 This is a good answer because it evaluates the photo for this enquiry by considering its **nature** and **purpose** and highlights issues about the impact on the audience.

Question 3(b): Identifying and explaining differences

Question 3(b) on your exam paper will ask you to identify 'the main difference between the views' in two interpretations. There are 4 marks available for this question.

Worked example

Study Interpretations 1 and 2 on page 36. They give different views about the causes of the success of the Montgomery Bus Boycott.

What is the main difference between the views?

Explain your answer, using details from both interpretations. **(4 marks)**

Remember to include points from both interpretations. It's important to refer directly to the interpretation and include short quotations to support what you say.

Spotting and explaining differences in interpretations

An interpretation is a historian's account or explanation based on evidence.
When analysing the differences between interpretations, think about the points of view the historians present. Look for the important or key differences, not just the surface details. For this question you need to look for a fundamental difference that you can spot.

 Links You can revise the Montgomery Bus Boycott on pages 4 and 5.

Sample answer

The historians disagree because Carson says the MIA was important in the success of the boycott. The other historian, Ling, says that King wasn't so important and it was the role of locals that made the campaign successful.

 This answer focuses on a surface point of difference rather than the underlying difference. A stronger answer would pick out a more fundamental difference.

Improved answer

Clayborne Carson argues that the boycott was successful because not only were the MIA members who organised the campaign committed to carrying on but also the lawyers who challenged segregation in the court succeeded. With Browder v. Gayle they 'struck down the legal basis for segregation'.

Ling's interpretation directly challenges the importance of King and the MIA. He argues that media coverage led to too much focus on King and not sufficient focus on other reasons for the successes, like Montgomery in 1955–56. Ling asserts that historians should be clearer about the importance of the localised nature of the struggles that King had a role in rather than placing him at centre stage. He points out that increasingly historians have insisted that the successes were as a result of a 'movement' not the achievements of 'one man'.

 Focus on the key point of difference, rather than on more minor differences.

 Use short quotations to support your analysis.

 You should explain a key difference and support it with detailed points from both interpretations.

 You must think about the specific language you can use in your answer, like: 'argues', 'claims', 'states', 'on the other hand' and 'backs this up'. These phrases help you produce a better answer because they help show you are analysing another person's judgement or opinion about something.

Question 3(c): Suggesting reasons for different views

Question 3(c) on your exam paper will ask you to suggest why two interpretations give different views. There are 4 marks available for this question.

Worked example

Links You can revise the Montgomery Bus Boycott on pages 4–5.

Suggest **one** reason why Interpretations 1 and 2 on page 36 give different views about the reasons for the success of the Montgomery Bus Boycott.

You may use Sources B and C on page 36 to help explain your answer.   **(4 marks)**

> You must give **one** reason why historians reach different conclusions about historical questions.

'Suggest' questions

In a question that asks you to suggest a reason, you need to offer and explain an idea about why there are differences. For example, interpretations might differ because they give different weight to different sources, because they aren't complete extracts, or because the authors have a different emphasis or focus. You need to show you understand that historical interpretations are judgements and opinions based on evidence and that, as a result, different views can exist.

Sample answer

Interpretations 1 and 2 give different views because the historians have different focuses.

Interpretation 1 focuses specifically on the events of the Montgomery Bus Boycott. Carson emphasises the connection between the activists boycotting the buses and the legal challenges in the courts. The idea that the boycott's success lay in this combined approach is supported by Source B, which shows the kind of racist hatred the campaigners faced, highlighting how difficult it was to bring about change.

Ling's focus in Interpretation 2 is wider. He places campaigns such as Montgomery within an assessment of the whole civil rights movement, emphasising how media campaigns that focused on key events and individuals like King may have distorted the bigger picture.

> You could explain the different views in the interpretations by looking at the different focuses the historians have chosen.

> Try to use at least one of the sources to support your argument about why the interpretations differ. This student uses Source B to support the idea that black Americans were subjected to racism.

> Make sure your explanation is clear and refers to **both** interpretations.

Question 3(d): Evaluating interpretations

Question 3(d) on your exam paper will ask you to evaluate an interpretation by explaining how far you agree with it. There are 16 marks available for this question. An additional 4 marks are available for good spelling, punctuation, grammar (SPaG) and use of historical terminology.

Worked example

How far do you agree with Interpretation 1 on page 36 about the reasons the Montgomery Bus Boycott was successful?

Explain your answer, using both interpretations and your knowledge of the historical context.

(16 marks plus 4 marks for SPaG and use of specialist terminology)

 **Links** You can revise the Montgomery Bus Boycott on pages 4–5.

How far do you agree?

You must:
- ✓ give detail from the interpretation to show that you understand the author's view
- ✓ provide detail from the historical context that supports the author's view
- ✓ consider how the interpretation is supported or challenged by the other interpretation and your own knowledge
- ✓ reach a judgement, giving reasons, about how far you agree with the view in the interpretation named in the question.

Sample extract

I agree that the boycotters did not give up. The boycott continued for 382 days and people were forced to walk to work through bad weather. Some of them had to walk for miles every day on top of doing their long hours at work. They also faced a lot of intimidation from white employers and racists in the city.

> The student gives a clear view but needs to refer more clearly to the interpretation they are discussing.

> The answer is not well developed because it lacks supporting evidence and only one interpretation is mentioned.

Improved extract

I agree with Interpretation 1 that the success of the Montgomery Bus Boycott was due to the 'perseverance' of the MIA members and the 'determination' of the lawyers who led the court case and defended Parks. However, Carson doesn't give sufficient credit to the importance of Martin Luther King, who raised funds for the MIA's activities and ensured the campaign got plenty of media coverage.

MIA members were vital to keeping the boycott going, even when the situation was really difficult. They received threats of violence against themselves and their families. So I agree with Interpretation 1 that their role was central to the success. It is also true that the boycott was supported by very determined lawyers, who launched a legal case in the courts as well as a defence case for Rosa Parks. This meant that, as stated in Interpretation 1, 'Browder v. Gayle (1956)... struck down the legal basis for segregation on Montgomery's buses'.

Interpretation 2 stresses the importance of smaller battles in which Martin Luther King did not take part, however I agree more with Interpretation 1. By focusing on Montgomery, the media perhaps exaggerated King's importance, but they publicised the whole issue and this was important.

> Highlighting key points in the interpretation can help you focus on the precise arguments that you need to evaluate to make your judgement.

> Try to challenge the emphasis put on the different factors under discussion and offer your own ideas.

> The student evaluates different points made in Interpretation 1, placing the arguments in the wider context, and goes on to comment on Interpretation 2.

> Remember that for this question 4 marks are available for good spelling, grammar, punctuation and use of historical terminology. Use specific historical vocabulary, such as: 'MIA', 'media coverage', 'segregation', 'boycott' and 'legal basis'.

Sources/Interpretations

These sources and interpretations are referred to in the worked examples on pages 32–35.

Source B: From a racist leaflet distributed by the White Citizens' Council (WCC) at a meeting in Montgomery, 10 February 1956. By this point the Mayor of Montgomery, W. A. Gayle, and several of his officials had joined the WCC.

> When in the course of human events it becomes necessary to abolish the Negro race, proper methods should be used. Among these are guns, bows and arrows, sling shots and knives. We hold these truths to be self evident that all whites are created equal with certain rights; among these are life, liberty and the pursuit of dead niggers. My friends, it is time we wised up to these black devils. I tell you they are a group of two legged agitators who persist in walking up and down our streets protruding their black lips. If we don't stop helping these African flesh eaters, we will soon wake up and find Rev. King in the White House.

Source C: Rosa Parks sitting at the front of a Montgomery bus on 21 December 1956, the day city buses were desegregated.

Interpretation 1: From 'To Walk in Dignity: the Montgomery Bus Boycott' by Clayborne Carson, published in the *Organisation of American Historians Magazine of History* (2005).

> The ultimate success of the boycott resulted not only from the perseverance of MIA members but also from the determination of the lawyers who challenged segregated bus seating in the courts. Clifford Durr worked closely with black attorney Fred Gray to provide legal defence for Parks and later advised NAACP attorneys involved in the Browder v. Gayle (1956) case that struck down the legal basis for segregation on Montgomery's buses, achieving the boycott's objective.

Interpretation 2: From an article by Peter Ling in *History Today*, Volume 48, Issue 4 April 1998.

> In recent years, however, historians have become unhappy with the distorting effect of the King legacy. The first sign of this discomfort, which reflects the misgivings of veterans of the Civil Rights movement, was the insistence that the movement was far more than Martin Luther King, Jr and that its achievements should not be ascribed to one man, however charismatic. More recently, this criticism has been enlarged by those scholars who have focused on the local struggles within which King was an occasional and sometimes marginal player.
>
> This has been particularly the case in studies of civil rights activism in Mississippi and Louisiana. For specialist historians, the television montage of the movement, which has King in the lead role of a thirteen- or fourteen- year epic from 1954–55 to 1968, because of its emphasis on the 'war reports' from Montgomery in 1955–56 to the Selma-to-Montgomery march of 1965, fails to capture vital aspects of what made the movement possible and successful.

Practice

Put your skills and knowledge into practice with the following question.

> **Option 33: The USA, 1954–75: conflict at home and abroad**

SECTION A

Answer questions 1 and 2.

Source A: Draft resisters at a demonstration in Washington DC arranged by the National Mobilization Committee to End the War in Vietnam, 1969.

1   Give **two** things you can infer from Source A about the anti-war movement in the USA from 1969 onwards.

Complete the table below to explain your answer.   **(4 marks)**

(i) What I can infer:

 Guided   From Source A I can infer ....

....

....

Details in the source that tell me this:

....

....

....

(ii) What I can infer: ....

....

....

....

Details in the source that tell me this:

....

....

....

You have 1 hour 20 minutes for the **whole** of Paper 3, so you should use the time carefully to answer all the questions fully. Remember to leave 5 minutes or so to check your work when you've finished writing.

🔗 **Links** You can revise opposition to the Vietnam War on pages 21 and 22.

Spend about 5 minutes on this answer. Identify **two** valid inferences from the source.

To 'infer' is to make a claim based on evidence: in this case, the source you are given in the exam.

An example of a suitable inference might be that 'The anti-war movement included those men who had been called up to join the US army to fight in Vietnam, but who refused to go.'

You need to give supporting details selected from the source to back up both your inferences.

Practice

Put your skills and knowledge into practice with the following question.

2 Explain why the USA escalated their involvement in Vietnam under Johnson, 1963–69.

You may use the following in your answer:

- Vietcong built complex tunnel networks
- the Gulf of Tonkin incident

You **must** also use information of your own. **(12 marks)**

Guided There are a number of reasons why Johnson escalated the war

....

....

....

....

....

....

....

....

....

....

....

....

....

....

....

....

....

....

....

....

....

 You have 1 hour 20 minutes for the **whole** of Paper 3, so spend about 18 minutes on this answer.

 'Explain' means you have to give causes of the escalation of US involvement in the Vietnam conflict, not just describe what happened.

You need to include information of your own that is not in the bullet point hints.

 Links You can revise the escalation of the Vietnam War under Johnson on pages 18–19.

 Marks are awarded for your analysis and understanding of causation and for your knowledge and understanding of the topic.

 Useful phrases when answering causation questions include: 'because', 'led to', 'resulted in', 'propagated', 'factors that caused'.

 Keep your explanations focused on the question. Although you might remember lots of detail about the Vietnam War, you need to focus on providing reasons why the US escalated their involvement in the conflict, not on giving a description of it.

Practice

Use this page to continue your answer to question 2.

....
....
....
....
....
....
....
....
....
....
....
....
....
....
....
....
....
....
....
....
....
....
....
....
....
....
....

You need to show a good knowledge of the key features and characteristics of the event and analyse causation. You also need to show how factors combined to bring about an outcome – in this case, how different factors came together, resulting in the escalation of US involvement in Vietnam.

Practice

Use this page to continue your answer to question 2.

....

....

....

....

....

....

....

.... ⟵ You must include a conclusion to sum up how the different causes led to this event.

....

....

....

....

....

....

....

....

....

....

....

Practice   Had a go ☐ ....

....

....

Practice

Put your skills and knowledge into practice with the following question.

SECTION B

3 (a) Study Sources B and C on page 49.

How useful are Sources B and C for an enquiry into the beliefs and methods of Malcolm X?

Explain your answer, using Sources B and C and your knowledge of the historical context.　　**(8 marks)**

Guided　Both Sources B and C are useful for finding out

about the beliefs and methods of Malcolm X in the civil

rights movement

....

....

....

....

....

....

....

....

....

....

....

....

....

....

....

....

....

....

....

....

....

....

You should spend about 12 minutes on this answer.

'How useful' means you have to judge what the sources suggest about the enquiry question and what the limits or problems could be.

Links　You can revise Malcolm X's ideas and tactics on page 12.

You need to identify and comment on the pros and cons of each source and make a judgement.

Make sure you include some knowledge of the context and don't just rely on information given in the sources.

Practice

Use this page to continue your answer to question 3(a).

Guided However, there are some drawbacks with both sources for this enquiry. These include

Remember, you need to evaluate the usefulness of both sources.

Practice

Put your skills and knowledge into practice with the following question.

3 (b) **Study Interpretations 1 and 2 on page 50. They give different views about the beliefs and methods of Malcolm X.**

What is the main difference between these views?

Explain your answer, using details from both
interpretations.   **(4 marks)**

 You should spend about 5 minutes on this answer.

 Links You can revise Malcolm X on page 12.

Guided   Interpretations 1 and 2 both discuss Malcolm X

but offer different views about ....

 You need to identify the key difference, rather than just surface differences.

....

....

....

 Make sure you refer to both interpretations.

....

....

....

 Remember, historians' interpretations offer **their** views and opinions about causes, events and significance.

....

....

....

 Remember to focus on the underlying **difference**.

Practice

Put your skills and knowledge into practice with the following question.

3 (c) Suggest **one** reason why Interpretations 1 and 2 on page 50 give different views about the beliefs and methods of Malcolm X.

You may use Sources B and C on page 49 to help explain your answer.   **(4 marks)**

Guided   Interpretations 1 and 2 offer different views
....
because
....
....
....
....
....
....
....
....
....
....

You should spend about 5 minutes on this answer.

You need to explain **one** reason why the interpretations differ.

You can revise how to analyse interpretations on page 29.

Focus on **why** the views are different. Think about whether the historians are giving different weight to different sources, whether they are using incomplete extracts, or if they have a different emphasis or focus.

Make sure you refer to **both** the interpretations to back up your answer.

Remember, historians' interpretations are **their** views and opinions about causes, events and significance.

Practice

Put your skills and knowledge into practice with the following question.

Up to 4 marks of the total will be awarded for spelling, punctuation, grammar and use of specialist terminology.

You should spend about 30 minutes on this answer.

3 (d) How far do you agree with Interpretation 1 on page 50 about the beliefs and methods of Malcolm X?

Explain your answer, using both interpretations and your knowledge of the historical context. **(20 marks)**

You can revise how to analyse and evaluate interpretations on page 29.

Guided | .... with the views in Interpretation 1

You need to provide a clear line of argument. Say whether you agree or disagree in the first sentence.

....

....

....

....

....

....

Say why you think the interpretation is valid or questionable.

....

....

....

Remember that 4 marks are for **SPaG** in this question. Make sure you leave time to check your spelling, punctuation and grammar.

....

....

....

....

Make sure you refer clearly to your **own knowledge** of the historical context.

....

....

....

....

....

....

....

....

....

Practice

Use this page to continue your answer to question 3(d).

....

....

....

....

....

....

Remember, historians' interpretations offer **their** views for you to challenge.

....

....

....

....

....

Give further reasons why you think the interpretation is valid or questionable.

....

....

....

....

....

Make sure you refer to both the interpretations to back up your answer.

....

....

....

....

....

Include a number of reasons for your opinion in order to build an argument throughout.

....

....

....

....

....

....

....

....

Practice

Use this page to continue your answer to question 3(d).

Practice

Use this page to continue your answer to question 3(d).

....

....

....

....

....

....

....

....

....

....

....

....

....

....

....

....

....

....

....

....

....

....

....

....

....

....

....

Include a brief conclusion to sum up your argument.

Sources/Interpretations Booklet 1

Sources B and C for use with Section B questions on pages 41–48.

Source B: From a speech made by Malcolm X in November 1963.

If violence is wrong in America, violence is wrong abroad. If it is wrong to be violent defending black women and black children and black babies and black men, then it is wrong for America to draft us and make us violent abroad in defense of her. And if it is right for America to draft us, and teach us how to be violent in defense of her, then it is right for you and me to do whatever is necessary to defend our own people right here in this country.

So I cite these various revolutions, brothers and sisters, to show you that you don't have a peaceful revolution. You don't have a turn-the-other-cheek revolution. There's no such thing as a non-violent revolution. The only kind of revolution that is non-violent is the Negro revolution. The only revolution in which the goal is loving your enemy is the Negro revolution. It's the only revolution in which the goal is a desegregated lunch counter, a desegregated theater, a desegregated park, and a desegregated public toilet; you can sit down next to white folks – on the toilet. That's no revolution. Revolution is based on land. Land is the basis of all independence. Land is the basis of freedom, justice, and equality.

Source C: African-American women grieving for Malcolm X after his assassination, Faith Temple, New York City, USA, 27 February 1965.

Sources/Interpretations Booklet 2

Interpretations 1 and 2 for use with Section B questions on pages 43–48.

Interpretation 1: From the article 'Malcolm X's assassination robbed the world of a Muslim civil rights visionary' by Tim Stanley, which appeared in *The Telegraph* on 20 February 2015.

> So why, then, has Malcolm's reputation among historians improved dramatically since the years following his assassination? Partly, his biography became better understood. In 1963–64, Malcolm began to split with the Nation in an argument over personalities and tactics – and in the few months that he still had to live there was a revolution in his politics. Critical to this was Malcolm's conversion from the Nation of Islam to mainstream Sunni Islam. He went on a pilgrimage to Mecca and was struck by the racial harmony among Muslims: "There were tens of thousands of pilgrims, from all over the world. They were of all colors, from blue-eyed blonds to black-skinned Africans. But we were all participating in the same ritual, displaying a spirit of unity and brotherhood that my experiences in America had led me to believe never could exist between the white and non-white."

Interpretation 2: From the history website history.com.

> The almost painful honesty that enabled him [Malcolm X] to find his way from degradation to devotion to his people, the modest lifestyle that kept him on the edge of poverty, and the distance he somehow managed to put between himself and racial hatred serve… as poignant reminders of human possibility and achievement.
>
> Influenced largely by Malcolm, in the summer of 1966 members of SNCC called for black power for black people. Their lack of power was the foundation of Malcolm's charge that they were denied human rights in America. His clarity on this matter, as America continues its retreat from its commitment to full freedom for his people, has guaranteed for him pride of place among black leaders.

Answers

Where an exemplar answer is given, this is not necessarily the only correct response. In most cases there is a range of responses that can gain full marks.

SUBJECT CONTENT

Civil rights, 1954–60

1. The early 1950s

For example:

Bad treatment of black Americans in the early 1950s	Organised resistance to bad treatment
• Formal segregation ensured by 'Jim Crow' laws • Public facilities such as hospitals and schools segregated • Black Americans viewed as racially inferior by white Americans • Racist attacks not properly dealt with by the authorities • Black Americans banned from juries • White gangs used violence and intimidation to stop black Americans from voting • Laws were used to stop black Americans from voting, such as the introduction of a literacy test they needed to pass before they could vote; black Americans struggled to pass this test	• Congress of Racial Equality (CORE) set up in 1942 • CORE used non-violent direct action • NAACP (National Association for the Advancement of Colored People) established in 1909 • NAACP used the courts to fight for civil rights

2. Brown v. Topeka, 1954

The *Brown v. Topeka* (1954) legal case was significant in a number of ways. Firstly, the case generated a lot of publicity about segregation in education and increased awareness of the civil rights campaign. The Supreme Court verdict was a huge boost to the campaign for civil rights, which encouraged campaigners to continue to challenge segregation laws. However, there were negative outcomes too. For example, segregation continued by other means, and many white families moved to new neighbourhoods where fewer black Americans lived and attended local schools. Also, black students who attended the newly integrated schools were treated badly and faced threats and violence from racist white Americans. Therefore, overall the *Brown* case was significant, as it spurred on calls for desegregation while also revealing the extent of opposition to desegregation in the Southern states.

3. Little Rock High School, 1957

- The NAACP wanted to ensure that desegregation was actually happening in schools after the Supreme Court rulings of 1954–55. Little Rock was an opportunity for campaigners to test out what happened when black students attended newly desegregated schools.
- Orval Faubus was a fierce opponent of desegregation, so his actions in using state troops gained a lot of negative publicity and encouraged support for those who wanted desegregation. The terrible treatment of the black students, who were racially attacked, shocked Americans living outside the Southern states.
- President Eisenhower was forced to get involved and take action to protect the black students, as America's global reputation was being damaged by the events at Little Rock. The US wanted to present itself to the world as a democracy, and negative publicity about racial discrimination was out of step with that image.

4. The Montgomery Bus Boycott, 1955

1 For example:
- She was a positive figurehead for the campaign.
- She was a political activist who was secretary of the local NAACP.
- She was an experienced campaigner who knew how to protest using non-violent direct action.

2 For example:
- Secure organisation of the campaign through the MIA: this meant the campaign had a clear strategy, for example, the use of car pools.
- Media coverage: this meant public support for the campaign grew as more Americans became aware of what was happening. This led to increased support in the North from white Americans, who were appalled by the treatment of black Americans in the Southern states.
- Non-violent direct action: this meant the campaign gained more support from white and black Americans, as the activists were seen to be peaceful and acting with moral integrity.

5. Importance of the boycott

Your concept map could include the following points:
- King emerged as a clear leader in the civil rights movement as a result of the Montgomery campaign, for which he was a figurehead.
- The Montgomery Bus Boycott led to increased popular support for the civil rights movement in general, and this influenced the passing of the 1957 Civil Rights Act.
- NAACP was successful in getting the Supreme Court to rule that bus segregation was unconstitutional (against the 14th Amendment), as the *Brown* ruling had established a legal precedent for this.

6. Opposition to civil rights: the KKK and violence

For example:

- Emmett Till was accused of harassing and making sexual advances to a white woman. This type of accusation commonly led to black Americans being targeted, often by the Ku Klux Klan, who wanted to 'protect' white Americans from 'black threats'.
- Emmett Till's murder was very violent: he was savagely beaten to death rather than being tried in a court of law for the crime he was accused of.
- The outcome of Emmett Till's murder was typical, as the white defendants were rarely prosecuted for their crimes. In this case they were let off and actually profited from selling their story. Many police officers and judges in the South supported or sympathised with the aims of the Ku Klux Klan.

7. Political opposition to desegregation

For example:

- Set up White Citizens' Councils
- Physically attacked black Americans who challenged segregation
- Shut down schools that were due to integrate
- Anti-integration politicians (the 'Dixiecrats') blocked civil rights legislation
- Organised pro-segregation protests

Protest and progress, 1960–75

8. Greensboro and the sit-in movement

For example:

G reensboro sit-ins, started by

R ichmond, Blair, McCain and McNeil

E ncouraged others to join the campaign

E nlarged to 50 000 in sit-in movement by 1960

N orth Carolina was the starting point for this movement

S outhern states, 'Jim Crow' laws challenged in the campaign

B lack and white Americans campaigned together to

O verturn segregation in public places such as

R estaurants and lunch counters

O thers found out more about the campaign from widespread media coverage of the protests

9. Progress in civil rights, 1960–62

In 1956, the Supreme Court had already ruled that state transport had to integrate, however, bus station toilets and waiting rooms remained segregated. So, in December 1960, progress was made when the Supreme Court ordered desegregation of bus station facilities to remove this loophole. In 1961, CORE and SNCC activists organised bus journeys through the Deep South to test whether desegregation was happening on the ground and if the Supreme Court rulings had really made a difference. They wanted to make federal government take action by putting pressure on the politicians. Through the Freedom Rides, campaigners generated lots of publicity about desegregating bus station facilities, which helped to advance their cause. However, they also faced violence, such as the Anniston bombing on 14 May 1961, which shows that progress was limited and would continue to be hard fought.

10. Peaceful protests and their impact, 1963–65

For example:

Impact of the Birmingham campaign:

- Bull Connor's treatment of protesters generated a lot of negative media attention and helped gather sympathy for the civil rights movement.
- The Birmingham campaign had impact on Kennedy, who became determined to pass a Civil Rights Act.

Impact of the March on Washington:

- King made his famous 'I have a dream' speech, which became one of the most recognisable calls for civil rights activism from the period.
- At that time it was the largest ever protest in the USA, which showed the support for civil rights by the marchers who attended, both black and white Americans.

Impact of the Mississippi Freedom Summer:

- The campaign was successful as thousands of black citizens signed up to vote.
- The murder of three activists by the Ku Klux Klan showed that violent opposition was still a very real possibility for campaigners.

11. Civil rights law, 1964–65

President Kennedy: Had an important role as he gave high-level jobs to African Americans, such as Thurgood Marshall. He supported the introduction of new civil rights laws but was assassinated before he could complete the measures in law. In Mississippi he sent federal troops to ensure that James Meredith could enrol at the University of Mississippi. He also supported federal escorts for the Freedom Riders, to ensure their safety.

President Johnson: He carried on some of the progress made by Kennedy and initiated some improvements himself. He continued to appoint black people to high-level jobs, including US Ambassador Patricia Harris. He saw through the 1964 Civil Rights Act and 1965 Voting Rights Act. He made federal interventions in 1965 to escort protesters marching from Selma to Montgomery.

12. Malcolm X

For example:

> In prison Malcolm X joined the Nation of Islam (NOI) and became their spokesman and supported black nationalism.

> He was an effective public speaker and helped increase support for the NOI and raised awareness of inequality and approaches to challenge it.

> He rejected non-violent direct action as ineffective and advocated black self-defence as an alternative.

> He related well to angry young people in Northern US cities.

> He left the NOI as he began to challenge their ideas and set up the Muslim Mosque, Inc. (MMI). He went on a pilgrimage to Mecca and rejected many of his old beliefs about separatism.

> He came to believe integration with white Americans could be possible, and met with other organisations including SNCC and CORE and set up the Organization of Afro-American Unity (OAAU).

13. Black Power, 1963–70

For example:

Black Power ideas	Black Power achievements
• Believed non-violent methods were too slow and had limited impact • Believed black Americans should not try to adapt to white society, as it would always seek to make them second-class citizens • Thought they should demand change rather than negotiate change with white Americans • Sought self-respect for black Americans based on pride and an awareness of their history as a people • Concerned with wider social issues and inequalities	• Smith and Carlos using the Black Power salute at the 1968 Mexico Olympics gained worldwide attention to the cause of black Americans • Provided a set of fresh ideas about challenging the inequalities in the USA that many black people could relate to • Focused on local and often social and economic problems that were real and meaningful to black people's lives

14. The civil rights movement, 1965–75

In 1966, King moved the focus of his campaigning to the North. Initially he found it difficult to fully understand the problems and people in the Northern cities and the ghettos. He decided to start a campaign for fairer housing, as this was central to the needs of Northern black Americans. However, riots broke out and media coverage of these had a bad effect on King's cause and message. King's outspoken criticism of the USA's involvement in Vietnam also meant President Johnson was less supportive of him. In 1968, King was assassinated. The 1968 Civil Rights Act was passed, which focused on fair housing and federal protection for civil rights workers, the issues that King had recently been promoting. Some white Americans mistakenly took that as meaning the civil rights struggle was over, especially since the Civil Rights Act (1964) and Voting Rights Act (1965) had already been passed. King's death also meant that white support for civil rights diminished, as the movement had benefited from having King as a figurehead that white Americans could trust and who was viewed as a moderate.

15. Civil rights achievements up to 1975

For example:

Progress made in civil rights, 1965–75	More progress needed
• Nixon supported black employment policies and encouraged affirmative action • Increased training opportunities for black Americans • 1970 Voting Rights Act banned literacy tests across USA	• Desegregation did not actually guarantee improvements in schools and public services for black Americans • Nixon presented promotion of black home ownership as a way to stop blacks destroying property • Nixon presented improved civil rights as an opportunity to gain control of the black population rather than as an issue about justice and equality

War in Vietnam, 1954–75

16. US involvement in Vietnam, 1954–61

For example:

- The USA supported the French against the Vietminh to stop the spread of communism in the region.
- The French were struggling so the USA increased its funding and, by 1954, it was paying 80 per cent of the cost of France's war.
- After the French left Vietnam, the USA wanted to stop South Vietnam falling to the communists. It was influenced by the 'domino theory' – the idea that if one state in the region fell to communism then others would follow. This meant the USA set up SEATO, supported the government of South Vietnam and sent advisers to train the ARVN.

17. Kennedy and Vietnam, 1961–63

For example:

- Initially Kennedy wanted limited involvement in Vietnam to achieve his objectives. Therefore he continued with the policy of only sending advisers and financial support.
- After the Vietcong started making headway in 1963, Kennedy changed tactics to target the Vietcong. He again authorised the use of chemical weapons in Vietnam to destroy crops that were used by the Vietcong and to deforest jungle areas so the Vietcong had less cover to hide in.
- Kennedy also supported Diem's Strategic Hamlet Program of 1962, by which the ARVN moved villagers into fortified villages that were secure from Vietcong influence.

18. Escalation of the conflict under Johnson

For example:

Vietcong support was growing and getting stronger; the North Vietnamese and Chinese were helping the Vietcong. →The Gulf of Tonkin incident – two US naval ships were attacked, so Johnson used this as a reason to use armed force to defend South Vietnam and station US troops there. → The Ho Chi Minh Trail was increasingly used to get help and supplies to the Vietcong from North Vietnam.

19. Conflict in Vietnam, 1964–68

For example:

- The Vietcong planned ambushes against US troops and set simple, but deadly traps. Positive, as they did not need much specialist equipment.
- The Vietcong avoided open battles, preferring to sabotage roads and bridges to make it difficult for US troops to operate effectively. Positive, as the Vietcong avoided casualties that arose from fighting and hampered the progress of US troops.
- The Vietcong had strong support from ordinary Vietnamese villagers so were difficult to identify as a military threat. Negative, as ordinary people suffered and were targeted.
- The Vietcong used tunnels to store their supplies safely, hide securely and give medical assistance to the wounded. Negative, because as all supplies were stored together, they were easy to destroy if located by the enemy.

20. Changes under Nixon, 1969–73

For example:

1969: July – Nixon set out his new foreign policy called the Nixon Doctrine; implementing the Nixon Doctrine in Vietnam was called Vietnamisation.

1970: US troops were sent into Cambodia to stop communism spreading there from Vietnam.

1971: The USA supported the South Vietnamese invasion of Laos, to stop the spread of communism in that country.

1972: April – The USA began a heavy bombing campaign against North Vietnam.

Reactions to Vietnam, 1964–75

21. Reasons for the growth of opposition

For example:

- The student population, which was influenced by the anti-war movement, rose significantly in numbers in this period.
- Vietnam was the first war where reporters accompanied soldiers onto the battlefield and reported back on what they saw happening.
- The advent of mass TV ownership meant people saw information about the war on a daily basis in their living rooms.
- Young people were often angry about the system by which men were drafted into the armed forces to fight in Vietnam.
- The extensive media coverage in newspapers and TV meant the American public acquired a deeper understanding of the issues in the war and questioned its validity.

22. Continued opposition to the war

There are a number of reasons why opposition to the Vietnam War grew. These include the media, the actions of the army leaders and soldiers on the ground, and how the Vietnamese people were treated. The war in Vietnam was covered in media reports to an extent that no other conflict had been reported. This meant people were better informed and no longer just relied on government information or propaganda about the war. Decisions made by army leaders and the government, such as the use of chemical weapons in Vietnam, were seen as very controversial and led to strong opposition to the war. Soldiers on the ground sometimes questioned the war themselves and lost heart about what they were doing, especially when the treatment of ordinary Vietnamese peasants was so harsh and they lost their lives and homes. Some senseless massacres of women and children took place, such as at My Lai, and this further increased hostility to the war.

23. Support for the Vietnam War

President Nixon, my support for the war is based on my love for this great country, the USA. We must stop the communists and their attempt to take hold of large areas around the world, which harms the USA's interests. We are a proud nation, which fights for freedom and must never accept defeat. Our standing on the world stage will be greatly diminished by a defeat, which must never happen. The anti-war protesters are un-American and should be ashamed of how they represent the USA to the world. Hard-working Americans support the war. They know the meaning of sacrifice and determination.

24. The peace process and end of war

For example:

- The USA was keen to withdraw from Vietnam as quickly as possible and so it agreed to a deal that did not properly protect South Vietnam's future.

- The South Vietnamese economy was in ruins due to a combination of a loss of US revenue after their withdrawal and bad rice harvests. The government could not secure enough support, so the villagers came under the influence of the Vietcong again.

- The North Vietnamese wanted a united, communist Vietnam. North Vietnam gave up waiting for Thieu to negotiate. They started fighting again in late 1974. The ARVN could not fend off the attack, but Congress would not approve funds to provide help. Saigon fell to the communists in April 1975.

Reasons for US failure in Vietnam

25. The strengths of North Vietnam

For example:

Political advantages	Geographical advantages	Cultural advantages
• Ideological commitment to the war • No challenge to the aims of the North Vietnamese government by the people	• Great knowledge and understanding of the jungle environment • Used to living and fighting in these sorts of jungle conditions • North and South Vietnam had been unified in the past and had good knowledge and understanding of each other's countries as they were still direct neighbours	• All people expected to take an active role in the conflict, including the old, the young and women • North Vietnamese believed they were fighting as a matter of honour

26. The weaknesses of US armed forces

The main weaknesses were lack of money, training and support for the war. There was the continuing problem that Congress was reluctant to provide more and more funding for an unpopular war. By 1971 they had cut the budget, which had a direct impact on resources needed for fighting the war effectively. The military strategy used was questionable and based on misunderstandings and a lack of knowledge of the Vietnamese people and culture. The US military was unclear about how to defeat their enemy and the methods needed to counter guerrilla-style warfare. As a result, US troops, often young and inexperienced, lacked the relevant training. These problems, together with lack of support for the war at home, led to low morale among the troops.

27. Impact of US opposition to the war

For example:

- The USA was more divided in various ways. Domestic issues had been neglected due to resources going to fight the Vietnam War instead, and the war did not unite the American people; rather it created tensions and led to more distrust of the government and military.

- The position of the US government and its reputation for protecting democratic values was damaged. People no longer trusted the government and politicians as they had previously.

- The USA was less sure of itself as a country. War veteran suicide rates were high and old certainties, such as Americans having unquestioning patriotism, were no longer there.

PRACTICE

37. Practice

1 (i) What I can infer: From Source A I can infer large numbers of people mobilised to campaign against the war in Vietnam.

Details in the source that tell me this: The details in the source that tell me this are that the demonstration was arranged by the National Mobilization Committee to End the War. By refusing to accept the draft their aim was to make the war impossible to continue.

   (ii) What I can infer: From Source A I can also infer that the demonstrators took their national campaign to the political centre of the country. They clearly sought to speak directly to the politicians who made policies about the war.

Details in the source that tell me this: The details in the source that tell me this is the fact that the demonstration took place in Washington DC.

38. Practice

2 There are a number of reasons why Johnson escalated the war. These include the strength of the Vietcong and the tactics they deployed. Also, the degree of domestic support that he secured, which was helped by the Gulf of Tonkin incident to some degree and the extent to which the Vietcong were getting foreign help in the war. Johnson wanted to stop communism spreading in the region and was sure that defeat of the Vietcong was vital to this end.

A key reason for the escalation of the war was that in August 1964 North Vietnamese boats attacked two US naval ships; this became known as the Gulf of Tonkin incident. The US carried out patrols using various ships including the *Maddox* and *C. Turner Joy*. The North Vietnamese were responding to the US carrying ARVN troops into North Vietnam to launch raids. Johnson used the incident against the navy as a reason to use armed force to defend South Vietnam and station US troops there. He also passed the Gulf of Tonkin resolution, which stopped short of a declaration of war against North Vietnam but in effect had the same outcome.

Another significant reason for the escalation of the war was Vietcong tactics, including tunnels. They were used to store weapons and supplies and as a means to escape when needed. The Vietcong could keep close to their US enemy and had a place from which to organise their ambushes. They managed to win strong support from locals who might cover for them. The Vietcong guerrilla-war-style tactics were hard to defeat. The might of the US armed forces was not very effective against these tactics. This meant that Johnson felt the war needed to be escalated so he could find a means to defeat the Vietcong.

In addition, Vietcong support was growing and getting stronger, with the North Vietnamese and Chinese giving help including soldiers and weapons. The Ho Chi Minh Trail was increasingly used to get help and supplies to the Vietcong; this network of paths and smaller trails stretched between Laos and Cambodia and North Vietnam. Over time the paths became wider and easier to use to send more support.

Johnson wanted to establish a South Vietnamese government that was strong and well supported by the people. However, the government of South Vietnam was in fact weak and hated by the people, it needed greater support from the USA to survive. All these factors encouraged Johnson to escalate US involvement in Vietnam.

41. Practice

3 (a) Both Sources B and C are useful for finding out about the beliefs and methods of Malcolm X in the civil rights movement. Source B is an extract of a speech made by Malcolm X. As such it provides a clear insight into his ideas and how he presented these to the listening public. In the speech he challenges the idea that black draftees should be forced to fight in Vietnam on the grounds that black Americans face violence at home. Malcolm X was drawing comparisons in order to draw attention to the hypocrisies that existed in the USA. This was an important method that he adopted, as it helped people to understand his argument about how black Americans should see their situation and how they should act about it. Malcolm X also undermines King's position about non-violence and the Christian idea of 'turning the other cheek'. The speech is useful because it

allows us to see how Malcolm X disagreed with other philosophies in the movement and how he explained his particular viewpoint.

The photo (Source B) is in some ways less useful for this particular enquiry, as it does not give us the actual words. However, it does show how his devoted supporters received Malcolm X's death and this suggests that he was a significant individual because of what he brought to the movement. The photo was taken in 1965 just after his assassination. He was killed by the Nation of Islam as he became their adversary after he left their group and began to find his own path for leading in the civil rights struggle. The photo is from 'Faith Temple' in New York. After leaving the NOI, Malcolm X became more open to working with other groups and more tolerant of the international Muslim community.

However, there are some drawbacks with both sources for this enquiry. These include the fact that we are not sure who Malcolm X's specific audience was. If it was his closet supporters rather than the general public, that might have affected the way he explained points and how he wanted to come across in terms of how activists should take action.

43. Practice

3 (b) Interpretations 1 and 2 both discuss Malcolm X but offer different views about his beliefs and methods. The central difference in the two interpretations is that Interpretation 2 defends Malcolm X's black nationalism, saying that black Americans were 'denied human rights in America' and that Malcolm's ideas fuelled the call for 'black power for black people'. On the other hand, Interpretation 1 emphasises Malcolm's conversion to Sunni Islam and his move towards working with white people, as the Islamic pilgrims he encountered were 'of all colors, from blue-eyed blonds to black-skinned Africans'.

44. Practice

3 (c) Interpretations 1 and 2 offer different views because the historians have different focuses.

Interpretation 1 focuses on how Malcolm X's reputation has improved over time and Stanley highlights how Malcolm X changed his philosophy and approach in the year before he was killed.

However, Interpretation 2 emphasises Malcolm X's influence on the Black Power movement, focusing on his commitment to 'black power' and how his 'clarity' inspired others. Source B supports this idea because it gives evidence of Malcolm X's revolutionary ideas about black self-defence and the need for black power.

45. Practice

3 (d) I agree to some extent with the views in Interpretation 1. Stanley says that Malcolm X's biography was largely misunderstood, but that

his reputation has improved in recent years and that this is because the impact of his conversion from the Nation of Islam to being a Sunni Muslim is now better understood. Stanley says, in Interpretation 1, that Malcolm X had changed his mind and had come to believe that harmony between races was possible.

Interpretation 1 is questionable, however, because it pays too little attention to Malcolm X's ideas, methods and development. I think that Interpretation 1 exaggerates the importance of Malcolm X's transformation into a Sunni Muslim. An understanding of the context of Malcolm's life shows us he was the product of the racist violence he had experienced. He believed, for example, that the Ku Klux Klan had murdered his father, although no member was ever convicted of the murder. Hardly any Klan members were ever convicted for the murder of black Americans.

I know that Malcolm X did embrace the idea of Islam as an international religion after his pilgrimage to Mecca, but I know, too, that he did not give up his central commitment to black Americans taking charge of their own destiny rather than asking white society to help them.

Interpretation 2 puts Malcolm's ideas into context by remembering his early life and influences, and how these shaped his perspective on black Americans gaining civil rights. His impact on the Black Power movement is important and organisations like the SNCC still carried on working for 'black power for black people'.

Overall, I agree only a little with Interpretation 1. I think Malcolm X has to be remembered as a Black Power activist and also as a human rights activist. To over-emphasise changes in his position in 1963–64 is to forget his overriding contribution to the civil rights movement.

Notes

Notes

Notes

Notes

Published by Pearson Education Limited, 80 Strand, London, WC2R 0RL.

www.pearsonschoolsandfecolleges.co.uk

Copies of official specifications for all Pearson qualifications may be found on the website: qualifications.pearson.com

Text and illustrations © Pearson Education Limited 2017
Produced, typeset and illustrated by Tech-Set Ltd, Gateshead
Cover illustration by Kamae Design Ltd

The right of Victoria Payne to be identified as author of this work has been asserted by her in accordance with the Copyright, Designs and Patents Act 1988.

Content is included from Rob Bircher, Brian Dowse, and Kirsty Taylor.

First published 2017

20

10 9 8

British Library Cataloguing in Publication Data
A catalogue record for this book is available from the British Library

ISBN 978 1 292 16976 7

Printed in Slovakia by Neografia

Acknowledgements

The publisher would like to thank the following for their kind permission to reproduce their photographs:

(Key: b-bottom; c-centre; l-left; r-right; t-top)

Alamy Stock Photo: age fotostock 17b, Art Directors & TRIP 26c, Digital Image Library 9, Everett Collection Historical 12tc, 12br, 23cr, GL Archive 11l, 11r, 17t, Glasshouse Images 49, Granger Historical Picture Archive 10cr, 27tr, 36, IanDagnall Computing 21br, J. G. Domke 27br, vintageusa1 7, 25, ZUMA Press, Inc. 15; **Bridgeman Art Library Ltd:** 6t; **Getty Images:** Bettmann 8, David Fenton 13, 37, Francis Miller / The LIFE Picture Collection 3, Michael Ochs Archives 5, MPI 18, Photo 12 / UIG 4, UniversalImagesGroup 22; **Mary Evans Picture Library:** INTERFOTO AGENTUR 10t, Photo Researchers 30, The Everett Collection 6b, 14, 19, 21t, 23cl; **TopFoto:** The Granger Collection 1, 2

All other images © Pearson Education

Notes from the publisher

1. In order to ensure that this resource offers high-quality support for the associated Pearson qualification, it has been through a review process by the awarding body. This process confirms that this resource fully covers the teaching and learning content of the specification or part of a specification at which it is aimed. It also confirms that it demonstrates an appropriate balance between the development of subject skills, knowledge and understanding, in addition to preparation for assessment.

Endorsement does not cover any guidance on assessment activities or processes (e.g. practice questions or advice on how to answer assessment questions), included in the resource nor does it prescribe any particular approach to the teaching or delivery of a related course.

While the publishers have made every attempt to ensure that advice on the qualification and its assessment is accurate, the official specification and associated assessment guidance materials are the only authoritative source of information and should always be referred to for definitive guidance.

Pearson examiners have not contributed to any sections in this resource relevant to examination papers for which they have responsibility.

Examiners will not use endorsed resources as a source of material for any assessment set by Pearson.

Endorsement of a resource does not mean that the resource is required to achieve this Pearson qualification, nor does it mean that it is the only suitable material available to support the qualification, and any resource lists produced by the awarding body shall include this and other appropriate resources.

2. Pearson has robust editorial processes, including answer and fact checks, to ensure the accuracy of the content in this publication, and every effort is made to ensure this publication is free of errors. We are, however, only human, and occasionally errors do occur. Pearson is not liable for any misunderstandings that arise as a result of errors in this publication, but it is our priority to ensure that the content is accurate. If you spot an error, please do contact us at resourcescorrections@pearson.com so we can make sure it is corrected.